WINSLEY

FROM CECILIA TO VICTORIA

Winsley

from Cecilia to Victoria

BY

ROBIN AND BARBARA HARVEY

First published in the United Kingdom in 2007
by The Hobnob Press, PO Box 1838, East Knoyle, Salisbury SP3 6FA

British Library Cataloguing in Publication Data
A catalogue record for this book is available from the British Library.

ISBN 978-0-946418-62-6

Typeset in 11/13 pt Scala
Typesetting and origination by John Chandler
Printed in Great Britain by Salisbury Printing Company Ltd, Salisbury

Contents

Barbara and Robin Harvey arrived in Winsley nearly forty years ago, after escaping from London. They had grown up on opposite sides of that city and their paths only met a few years before that move. Barbara's great interest was in all to do with natural history, in flowers and gardening, and for many years she was in a research department with Kodak at Harrow. Robin, after his pre war school days at Dulwich College, followed his parents' mathematical tradition and read that subject at Cambridge University. This led, after war time service, much of it in the far east, to a lecturing career, eventually at Bath University. Retirement allowed us to indulge our interests in local history, especially in the recording of the vernacular buildings of the county. We have an abiding interest in music, and Robin recently gave up being secretary of the Methodist church here.

Prologue

S OME FIFTY YEARS AGO, the story of this village was gathered into a Scrapbook by the Winsley and Turleigh Women's Institute. After so long, if for no other reason, the time now seems ripe for attempting a more up to date version of that story. It is not surprising that over those years many new sources of information have emerged; among them, a number of important family archives have been deposited at the Wiltshire Record Office [W.R.O., now the Wiltshire and Swindon Record Office] and can be studied there. Naturally, too, much of the old story can now be seen from rather a different angle. Many details have become clearer since that Scrapbook was completed in 1957,[1] and it has become evident too that much of what was written about Winsley in Volume 7 of the Victoria County History of Wiltshire in the 1950s also needs revision in view of what has since come to light. One hopes that as large an advance in our knowledge will again be achieved when in due course another history will supersede this present one. Such a book will inevitably still contain its own errors. I can only beg your indulgence, dear reader, for any you may discover.

When my wife and I came to Winsley, the Tynings Estate had just begun to rise in the large field known as Hollybush Close. Our house deeds were our first introduction to an intriguing part of the village story. The picture widened when a few years later Ken Rogers, then County Archivist, and his wife Helen gave a series of evening lectures on the Wiltshire Landscape. They opened our eyes to a wealth of information about our new county and, among so much else, to those all important documents, the Tithe Apportionment (TA)[2] schedules and maps, and in particular what they tell about the local region a century and more ago. Innocently, we thought the coverage of these documents must be complete for all the country, but soon learnt that archives often contain awkward gaps. Obviously this led us to a tentative visit to the Record Office, to see what this mysterious document said about Winsley, its houses and fields. But further mysteries straightway appeared when the archivist whom Barbara approached asked her 'Do you want to see the Poor Rate Books too?' To that question the only possible answer then was 'What is a Poor Rate Book?' So here we attempt to tell where that and many other questions have led us.

Appearing in 1841, the Bradford Tithe Apportionment schedule provides a detailed picture of the town and its neighbouring villages, making that year a convenient starting point for searching out the history, looking both forwards towards the present and back into earlier times. For the happenings since 1841, we could not hope to match the story that real Winsley folk can tell from their own memories – perhaps this part of the story could better be termed 'current affairs'! The W. I. Scrapbook itself is of course a valuable source of these memories, since supplemented by 'Turleigh 2000', the book[3] which the people of that village compiled for the millennium bringing together its portrait, the flora, the life around it and much else. The present book is by contrast a personal selection of topics that look back in the opposite direction, back to the story of Winsley from earlier times up to the years around the Tithe Apportionment survey.

It is a pleasure to record our thanks to all those who have helped us in countless ways in the search for Winsley. First of all we thank those who compiled that W.I. book half a century ago, preserving so much material that would otherwise have been lost with the passing of the years, not to mention the fables then current. Grateful thanks, too, to the staff of the County Record Office who from that first visit onwards have so often drawn our attention to information about the village, guided our early uncertain steps and helped in many other ways. It would be invidious to give individual names. Thanks too to many friends in the village for help and encouragement, allowing us to consult their house deeds and to examine and record their homes. We owe a great debt too, to the Wiltshire Buildings Record, and in particular to Pam Slocombe, who introduced us to the pleasures of vernacular architecture in its many aspects. There are also the friends who have read earlier attempts, and whose valuable comments I have been glad to incorporate in the book as it has developed, – in the words of the old inventories, the 'things unseene and things forgot'. I am glad to thank Mrs Tracey Williams for her generous and expert help with correcting the text, not forgetting the vagaries of medieval spelling. And above all, there is the immense debt I owe to my late wife Barbara, for this book is of course our joint effort. Her collaboration, enthusiasm and detailed knowledge cannot be exaggerated, and I most gratefully dedicate the work to her memory.

Robin Harvey (Robert B. Harvey)

1
Introducing Winsley

W INSLEY has been a separate civil parish only since 1894, though it had become an ecclesiastical one in 1847. For centuries before that it had been a part of the old parish of Bradford on Avon [4]. In the middle ages the Abbey of Shaftesbury had a large estate and manor at Bradford, divided into a number of sections known as tithings centred on the surrounding villages, one naturally being the Winsley tithing. From the 12th century onwards the other tithings were Atworth, Holt, Leigh and Woolley, South Wraxall, Limpley Stoke, Trowle and of course the Bradford Borough itself. At some times, other

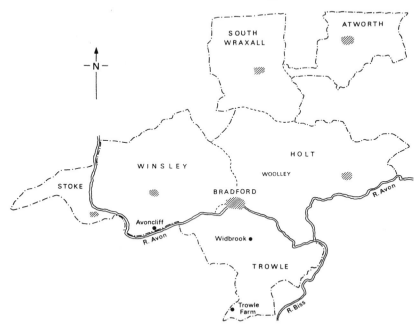

Bradford and its neighbourhood.

villages were also attached to this Bradford estate, only to be separated from it again later. At various periods, too, the two neighbouring tithings of Winsley and Stoke were closely associated, almost becoming a 'tithing of Winsley and Stoke'[5]. Another development in the middle ages was that important local families were able to gain a degree of independence from Bradford, acquiring sub manor status, but remaining basically subordinate to the main Manor of Bradford. This, however, seems not to have had much effect on our village.

For the purpose of this book, it is convenient to take 'Winsley', as well as being the name of the village, to mean that old tithing of Winsley, as it appears for instance in the 1841 Tithe Apportionment map – the one described in G. Langdon's book 'The Year of the Map'.[6] The main changes to the boundaries since then have been that Bradford town in its growth has swallowed sizeable pieces of the old Winsley, chiefly in the Newtown, Budbury and Bearfield areas. Like most of the other tithings, we have become a separate parish. Before 1842 it is more difficult to find out where our old Bradford boundary did lie. In the early part of the 17th century it probably ran along Newtown as far as the foot of Wine Street but to the west of that there are signs that there may still have

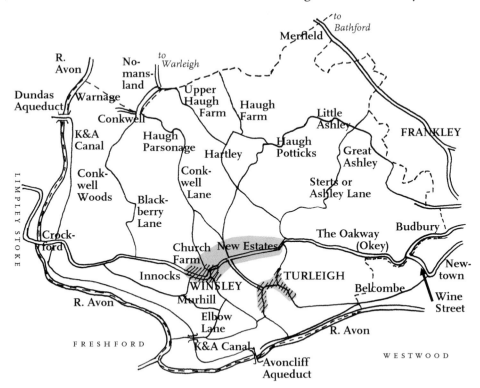

The Winsley tithing.

Looking across the Avon valley to Turleigh.

been an area where the land was held in common between the town and the Winsley tithing.

The name of the village has changed little over the years since its first appearance in writing in its latinised form 'Wineslega' around the year 1170. Names ending in -ley, spelt – legh, -lega or leah in earlier times, are of course common in most of England and refer to clearings in woodland; nowadays they are considered to belong most often to the later Saxon or Norman periods. So it is thought that Wine (pronounced Wina or Weena), a Saxon, left his name behind him at Winsley – Wina's Legh – and perhaps also at Wingfield (earlier Winefeld = Wina's field).[7] It used to be thought that the 'Wintresleu' named in the Domesday Book might have been Winsley, but that theory has been discarded for a century and more; the Domesday Wintresleu is now definitely known to refer to Winterslow, near the Hampshire border of Wiltshire. A more local red herring of a name is Winterleys or Winderles. The Tithe Map shows this was a large field, now split into several pieces, all of them south of the Avon, on the boundary between Bradford and Westwood. Clearly the name cannot be a forerunner of Winsley, though occasionally, for a few years around 1600 our village does sometimes appear as Wynnesley or even Wintersley.

Turleigh, the name of Winsley's sister village, on the other hand, is not a 'ley' name at all. Its earliest known occurrence in writing was at a comparatively late date, around 1350, its commonest medieval forms being Turlynge or Tyrlinge. The most likely meaning of the name seems still to be that found in

Green Lane, Turleigh.

The Place-names of Wiltshire in 1939.[8] This suggests that the name comes from a postulated Saxon word Thyrelung, meaning 'piercing', referring to the deep wooded valley we call Dane Bottom. Thyrelung would tie on to the name used in a single deed of 1418 [9], where Turleigh was written Thyrlynge [but this identification with Turleigh is itself rather suspect; it occurs in company with another one that is almost certainly wrong]. Dane, by the way, does not come from the ecclesiastical title, or from the invading Danes. It is the Saxon *denu*, a steep sided valley rising gently along its length. Because of the easy gradient leading up to higher ground, *denu* valleys often have roads running up them. A number of other derivations may be possible. For instance, a much earlier name that may possibly refer to Turleigh is found in a survey made by Shaftesbury Abbey[10] in the 1190s. In this survey we find some of the earliest mentions of the other Winsley hamlets like Ashley and Haugh, so it might be expected that Turleigh would be there too. Among the men of Winsley 'vill' we find men named Osbert, Adam and Heliot 'de Traveling' or ' de Traueling'. Could Traueling possibly be Turleigh? The connection of the two names is not clear, and it would need an expert on place names to assess the spelling changes needed to turn -ru- into -ur- (we can ignore the -a-, I think) and so make Trauelyng into Turlynge. And is it possible that this Trau- has survived as the Trows in Turleigh? This Turleigh problem gets a new twist each time one looks at it. So another thought arises from A.H.Smith's demonstration that the Saxon word 'trog' seems to have the primary meaning of a valley, as well as later becoming trough. Remembering that a late Saxon final 'g' was silent and not voiced, trog obviously gave us the Trows; but could it have given us Trog- linge for Turleigh as well?[11] From its medieval form, the development of the name is straightforward. By the early 17th century the name was usually written 'Tyrlinge alias Turlyn' [12] quoting both the old name and what was then the up-to-date one. Turlyn it remained all that century, but the 'n' dropped out in the 1700s. The final change from Turly into Turleigh, a bit of Victorian one-upmanship, did not happen till round the 1870s or 80s.

So far no mention of Murhill (Murrell) has been found before an Elizabethan Court Roll of the Parsonage Manor of Bradford. At this 'Curia Recognitionis' in 1563[13], the manor was bringing its tenants' records up to date. They confirmed that on the 12th of January 1553 William Guydyng – he probably lived at the cottage now No.155, Church Cottages – had been granted 'a Tenement (a holding) including a close of two acres of pasture called Murrells and two other closes ...' in Winsley. The first part of the name comes from the Saxon word (ge)maere, meaning a boundary, obviously referring to the county boundary along the river Avon. The same Saxon word also occurs in Merfield, the boundary field at the far end of the parish, towards Farleigh Wick. Winsley also includes the hamlets of Conkwell (the well on the Knock, i.e. hill) and Ashley (the ash-tree clearing)[14], and the region of more scattered farms at Haugh, nowadays pronounced Hay.. This last started as the Saxon 'gehaeg', a hedged clearing in the waste and woodland[15.] By the 12th century it was being written Hag', Agh, Ag', Haw or Hawey; in many parts of the country this sort of clearing would have been called an 'assart'. Men of Ashley and Haugh are mentioned in the Shaftesbury survey at that time, so those hamlets must date at least that far back.

Topography

WINSLEY, south east of Bath, is on a plateau, an outlier of the Cotswolds, which rises gradually from the outskirts of Bradford to a height of some 500 feet (150 metres) above sea level on the west, at Knowl (or Knoll) Hill above the Dundas Aqueduct, and with Conkwell nestling in its woods below. The River Avon forms Winsley's west and south boundaries. The steep slopes above it are now well wooded with a typical woodland flora where Herb Paris is fairly common. At the foot is meadow land, and in the pasture and arable above a number of native orchids have been found, even in some village gardens. Quite extensive quarries used to be active on the rock of the plateau. This 'Greater Oolite' limestone is good Bath stone, though Winsley stone is not as fine or hard as that from Combe Down and Corsham quarries.

Conkwell hidden in its woods, seen across the valley from Brassknocker Hill

J.T.Irvine's drawing of Conkwell.

It has clayish strata above it and on the spring line below, and other limestone strata lie still further underneath. North of Winsley itself the Geological Survey map seems to show a small cap of a rock called Forest Marble on top of the clay, and a wider band of the same from Hartley northwards. It makes soil that is easier to cultivate than the rather marshy clay just below it. In parts of the Cotswolds the Forest Marble was used for stone roofing tiles, and here we have records of a field called Tylepitts – a probable old name for Pit Close, at Upper Haugh Farm. It perhaps indicates that some stone tile making once went on in our part of the world too.

On this solid foundation there has been a constantly changing pattern of farms with their network of houses, fields and tracks. Particularly, within living memory the village itself has grown so much that it now consists of an 'old village', its area more than doubled by a group of new estates to the east. . Even on the 1901 Ordnance Survey map, the east end of the village was at the war memorial corner, apart from half a dozen houses scattered along the main road beyond Dane Bottom. In the countryside, too, the general picture has been changing as many old stone field walls have been removed to make way for larger fields and used for re-lining the canal. In fact, though, the present pattern differs comparatively little from that found on the 1841 Tithe Map. Before that, in 1727[16] a map was made for John Thresher, then lord of Winsley manor, to show in considerable detail the lands of his manor and of the Winsley

Parsonage which he also held, but leaving the rest of the parish blank. Many of the 1727 field boundaries were very like those of 1841, but hidden underneath our familiar fields, the map is full of clues to a much earlier and very different Winsley. Around the village itself this map divides the land into halves labelled North Field and South Field; in many places the medieval field strips are also carefully marked. Evidently these strips were still visible at that time and some may still have been cultivated in the old traditional way. This 1727 map seems to be the earliest Winsley one surviving; to take the story further back into the past we have to rely on descriptions in documents, each successive earlier picture of the parish retaining traces of the one that preceded it.

Let us look first at the village itself. There are many questions that can be asked about it, and very few that can be answered. Why, for a start, does it stand where it does? And how long has it been in its present position? Why did Winsley, rather than Turleigh or Haugh, grow into the chief settlement in the

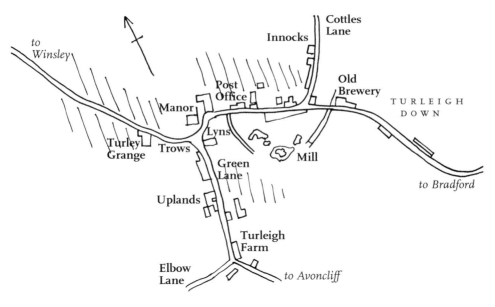

Turleigh map.

tithing? Then, we can ask about its plan – why is it not a linear village, spreading along the line of a main road, like Holt or Atworth[17], or a village grouped round its green? Every village has its own unique plan, but it is not easy to see how Winsley's present form fits into any of the standard models.

Why, then, was Winsley built where it is? To answer that, we would need to read the minds of the first inhabitants or the powers that be who first planted it here. What factors made them pick on this spot, this particular nook in the

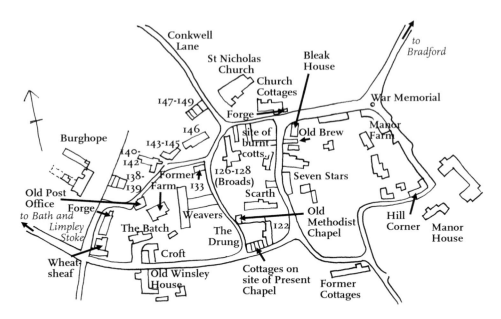

Old Winsley village.

woodland or corner of a newly cleared field for a house or two? Did they look primarily for a good water supply and a sheltered site? But isn't Turleigh better provided with that – on the spring line? Winsley's site may have had the advantage of better land for the crops or something like that. Perhaps the problem of defence came into it too, and its convenient distance from Bradford.

The plan of the old village roads has remained practically unchanged since the earliest maps we possess. To go from the Wheatsheaf crossroads at the west end to the Manor Farm on the east, we have a choice between two principal routes. The northern one, perhaps the older one following rather a zigzag path, is a lane which, perhaps significantly, first passes Burghope, its oldest part of great age, and then the sites of two ancient village features, the Pound, where straying animals were impounded, and the village Pond, roughly on the site of the Old Post Office. We know it was there at least since 1366[18] and no doubt long before. Then this lane passes the church and leads on out of the village past the Manor Farm. The other road we should perhaps, since the recent building of the village bypass, think of as the 'old main road'. Starting off eastwards from the Wheatsheaf cross roads, it turns north by the bowling green, and past the Seven Stars, to rejoin the first lane just east of the church. Or as a detour one can turn right at the bowling green corner and follow round to the south of it before turning north again at Hill Corner next to the Manor, regaining the main road outside Manor Farm. To complete the plan there is a

The Wheatsheaf corner. The Bath road goes off to the left. The Wheatsheaf House, behind the right hand cottage was the village bakery, butchery and shop. Bakery ovens still survive here and at No 122. We are told the baking oven used to be heated in early mornings by two bundles of faggots, and was then hot enough to bake two ovenfuls of loaves and two of cakes.

narrow path, a Drung, to give it its Old English name, running across between the two east-west roads. So the village is basically rectangular, with the north west corner cut off where some cottages have encroached onto the inner area. If we note, too, that on the 1841 Tithe Map most of the central area west of the Drung was occupied by one farmer, it is tempting to speculate and wonder if that whole central region was once a large village green.

Winsley used to have its forge, of course, and we can still see how it may have wandered during the last few centuries. At least three former forge buildings can be found – small extensions to the blacksmith's house next to the road. Forge Cottage at the north end of the cottage row next to the Wheatsheaf House had a single story added extension, apparently active as a forge in the early – mid 18th or perhaps into the later 19th century. Then at the other end of the village, on a survey by Edward Burcombe in 1754, someone scribbled a note about 1806, naming William Taylor,

The forge at no.155, Church Cottages.

blacksmith, together with James Eyles, as having The Blacksmith's Shop and the four cottages adjoining – now Church Cottages. And an obvious small detached forge stands against the road at the end of the row. The third and most recent forge was still working in living memory. Now the garage of no 123, Mr Organ is remembered for the iron hoops he used to make for the children of Winsley.

The story of the forges starts long before that, of course, for in the twelfth century, the Shaftesbury Abbey cartulary implies that even then there used to be a central forge in Bradford, but probably none in the surrounding villages. Around 1130, Ernewyn the smith paid the rent on his half virgate of land by maintaining the ironwork of the four manorial ploughs and by any other work he might be required to do. The manor was to give him the firewood for his furnace. By the end of the century there were two blacksmiths, Humfrey paying 12 pence for his forge in the town, and Walter at Wollewelle – was that Woolley?.

The lane out to Conkwell gives one a picture of the way our fields have developed. Starting next to the church, even before the lane has passed the churchyard, one reaches the gardens and houses of the recently built Late Broads estate on the left. This recent estate has buried the next section of the old lane, which used to run straight ahead, crossing the line of the bypass to go on northwards past Church Farm. The name Late Broads may sound odd, but it is easily explained. Before the estate houses were built, there was on the left of the road a large meadow of that name, stretching across as far as Burghope.[19] For most of the 18th century the house and this field belonged to a branch of the Broad family, and would naturally be called 'Broad's'. Then, when Alice Broad sold them in 1790, they became 'Late Broads', after the former owner, and the name has stuck.

Continuing across the bypass, the lane first ran north between a pair of fields, on the left one known as Burys or Berrys, lying in front of Church Farm,

The 1727 map reveals these curious markings in the Berrys just north of the village. What were they? The Church Farm is now just north east of the Berrys.

and one known as Bassetts Tyning on the right. The Berrys, nothing to do with blackberries, looks rather strange on the 1727 map, a muddle of a number of small patches of pasture separated by belts of woodland or scrub with what look like tracks running down the middle of them. There is no trace of these now. They lead into slightly wider, but still very small areas, perhaps indicating quarrying. In spite of the name, the map does not suggest there was an

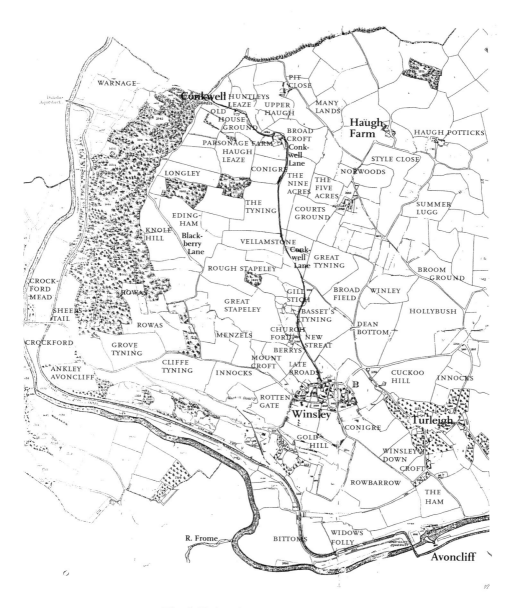

The fields beside the Conkwell Lane.

ancient burial or fortification here; it is equally unlikely to have been an old village site. Across the lane, Bassett's Tyning is easier to explain. A Tyning was an old English word for an inclosure – to tyne meant to inclose a piece of land for sowing a crop, in this case a piece of a medieval North Field which Richard Bassett inclosed around 1700[20]. A deed of 1715 records that Bassett mortgaged, among other things, 'all that new enclosed ground called the Tyning lying near the Church & containing 5 acres'. Assuming this refers to the present Bassett's Tyning, evidently Bassett was only mortgaging a part of his tyning, for the whole of it contains over 17 acres. Its northern boundary is along the lane that runs up from Beggars Bush to join the Conkwell Lane. Beggars Bush (does anyone still call it that?) was the point where Dane Rise meets Vinegar Path (now King Alfred Way). This lane[21] has a very thick wall on its northern side where they join, a sign perhaps of great age.

On the other side of the lane, northwards from Church Farm, the picture is rather different. The farm itself was built between 1825, when there was only a yard with a barn in it, and the 1841 Tithe map. I suspect Joseph Smallcombe of no. 146 bankrupted himself in the process. And a hundred years before the 1727 map shows – nothing there. The site used to be just the south corner of a long field called Gillstich or Kellstich along the side of the lane. Parts of this are remembered as marshy places where snipe used to be common. Gill, golden, could refer to bumper crops of buttercups here, and Stich[22] just means a piece or strip of land. It was in fact a long thinnish field, running along the side of the lane up as far as the junction with the Beggars Bush road. Half way along, one comes to the start of the footpath across to Blackberry Lane. There used to be a small paddock called New Street here, where the path turned off the lane. It nearly cut Gillstich in two. Winsley had several such fields with old 'Street' names, and this one dates back at least as far as John Kent's will in 1629[23]. Was it really a new street in Kent's time? However, the name, still in use on the 1727 map, had been forgotten by the beginning of the 19th century. Later maps just call it Paddock.

Looking along the footpath, there is a small coppice a short distance away. Formerly twice as large as now, the former eastern half was grubbed out – a 'breach' in the wood – hundreds of years ago and absorbed into Gillstich. It is my guess that it first became Coppice Breach, and that soon turned into Cock and Breeches as we find it on the tithe Map. Or does that name conceal some old village story?

To the west of the coppice lies Rough Stapeley, part of a vast field called Stapeley once stretching almost across to the main Winsley Hill road and westwards to Blackberry Lane. It has re-absorbed into itself half a dozen small pieces with names like Atkins' Stapeley and Bassett's Stapeley into which it was once split. Many villages have fields called Stapeley, i.e. Staple-legh, a staple being a pole or pillar, probably an early landmark. It has been suggested that Staples, being clearly marked by the post, were often used as places for holding local meetings or markets.

From this point on, the next stretch of the lane was unwalled till fairly recently. The 1727 map shows it as cutting diagonally across the old ploughing strips of Bellamstone or Vellamstone Field. This suggests that the old strip farming went out of use here before the road was moved to its present course. The 'Vellam' / 'Bellam' part of the name is unexplained, [24] but the 'stone' may alternatively have come from -tun, telling of a long vanished early farmstead.

The lane then leaves Winsley's old North Field and passes through the land of Parsonage Farm, where many of the fields bear early medieval names like Conyger and Besticles. Conyger, the rabbit warren, tells of the days when these 'conies' were first introduced into England by the Normans. In those days the law was that only big ecclesiastical or manorial estates were allowed to keep rabbits. There were two 'Conigers' in Winsley, [25] the other being next to what we now call the Manor House, but would then have been just Bradford manor's chief demesne farm in the Winsley tithing. That Conygre included the cricket ground and the area between that and the house. The one next to Parsonage Farm will date back to the origin of the Parsonage, as told in the second Shaftesbury survey of Winsley, made in about 1170 [26]. It relates that Cecilia, Abbess of Shaftesbury from 1107 to 1120, gave to the church at Bradford half a hide and a quarter of a virgate, say fifty or sixty acres of Winsley land. Over the centuries this gift was added to, I suppose by further grants, growing into a separate Rectory or Parsonage Manor, with our Parsonage Farm as one of its chief properties.

The final section of the road, turning west at this point as it approaches Conkwell, still has Parsonage land on its left, but on the right are fields of a different character, belonging to an area of enclosures reaching out along the northern boundary of the parish. These were cleared later than the original open fields, to meet the needs of a growing population. A careful examination of the Tithe Map seems to show that the cultivation of nearly all this northern area started as a number of these separate clearances – 'assarts' as they would be called – each of say 90 to 100 acres, roughly an old 'hide' of land. Others were about half that size. They reveal themselves by their rounded boundaries which other later, straighter ones often run up to but do not cross. Several of these assarts have old isolated farmsteads like Haugh Farm or Upper Haugh Farm in the middle. Others may well have grown round farms which have not survived. Each would be a separate encroachment into the waste, later divided into more manageable pieces by those straight walls and hedges.

It is worth looking again at Winsley's former open field farming system which the 1727 map revealed – what is often called a Ridge and Furrow system. In many villages, particularly in the heavy soil of much of the Midlands, these corrugated fields are easily seen to this day, but on the lighter soil of this part of Wiltshire the strips were more or less flat and nearly all their slight traces have been destroyed by the centuries of ploughing since the system went out of use[27]. The dividing line between Winsley's North[28] and South Fields seems to have run roughly north west and south east from the village. As well as being names on the map, these fields appear in dozens of indentures in the 17th and early 18th centuries. The map reveals how the arable land in these fields was divided into a multitude of long narrow strips which they called 'lands', These were say 8 yards (7½ m.) broad and of very variable length, the longest being about a furlong (that is 220 yards or say 200 m.) long. The evidence for this comes almost entirely from the map, but there one or two places in the parish where, if it is not wishful thinking, slight traces of these strips can still be seen. One is in Cliff Tyning (the Cleeves, i.e. the quarry), the big field on the south of the main road at the top of Winsley Hill, just west of the Avonpark entrance. After a light snowfall some of the furrows between the strips show up as white snowy lines just above the Winsley Nature Reserve. And there may be a few more to be seen near the southern fence of the cricket ground and elsewhere.

Sets of adjoining parallel strips usually came to be grouped together into what they then called 'furlongs'. It will be convenient to spell these with a capital F to avoid confusion with the modern meaning of the word. Around Bradford this word Furlong was often incorporated in the names of such groups

The old strip fields in Crockford at the bottom of Winsley Hill before the bridge was built.

of strips. In 1372, for instance[29], it was decreed that crops of oats were to be sown in Gavelfurlong and Wyggebroukesfurlong (Widbrook Furlong), but at Winsley the word does not seem to have been used in this way. Here Stapeley, which we have already met, was a Furlong containing groups of strips with various orientations, and Bellamstone, bigger than it now is, was probably another. Not so large was Warnage near Conkwell, which was divided into two parts, a Furlong with strips in Warnage Field and some meadow land below it in Warnage Mead next to the river. Above them are the woods below Conkwell. By the time the 1727 map was made, the strip system was dying and many landowners had managed to put together blocks of adjoining strips which could be farmed as a unit, a forerunner of the modern style field. So in Warnage there is a group of strips owned by Mr. John Long. Next to them on the south lay a group of eight manorial strips, followed by two belonging to John Blatchley, and so on. The War- part of the name comes from the Saxon for a weir across the river. Two questions therefore arise: was there ever a weir at Warnage, just downstream from the Dundas Aqueduct, and if there was, are there still any signs of it on the ground? Now a weir would be built for driving a mill, so one should be looking for traces of a mill hereabouts, but on which side of the river? There is of course a weir at Warleigh, a bit further downstream, with its mill at Claverton.

Another interesting Furlong is Crockford, with its partner Crockford Mead, next to the Stokesford bridge on the main road. Again the 1727 map shows the old arable strips with their owners. A few miles south of Warminster lies the village of Crockerton, which takes its name from a crocker, that is a potter; an ancient pottery industry flourished there until fairly recently. Our Crockford, however, is more likely to be named from the crooked ford there, for there seems to be no possibility of a pottery there. The geology is quite wrong for pottery. There has, too, been a great deal of disturbance of the ground here in the course of road and bridge building since 1727, as well as the construction of the canal, running right through that field. And the map shows that there was no bridge over the river at Crockford in 1727. The road down Winsley Hill did not have the present sharp turn downhill just above the canal bridge. Instead, it used to run straight on northwards across the field – it's called Sheepstails, but that's another story – following roughly the line of the canal to the meadows by the aqueduct at Warnage. In those days this road was in fact the main way to Warnage. There was, however, a trac leading down to the river between two of the strips in Crockford Field (number 24, belonging to Mr Thomas Dicke and number 21 to John Dawe). On reaching the river it turned right, leading to a ford a short distance downstream from the present bridge.

In July 1731,[30] shortly after this map was drawn, a group of the major landowners and inhabitants of Winsley came to an agreement with Thomas

Stokesford Bridge in the 19th century.

Dike of Limpley Stoke Manor and Moses Cottle the elder of Winsley – he lived at Winsley House, where Dorothy House now stands. It states that 'a bridge was intended to be built over the river Avon at or near ... Stokesford by the said Thomas Dike and Moses Cottle ... at their own proper costs'. It goes on to say that 'for some time past a way had been used across the river for Horses and Foot Passengers ... at Stokesford, but that some Doubts had arisen whether there is... any good Right of Way for such Passengers to go ... through the said Way'. It had been agreed that 'it would be deemed to become a Publick and Common Highway Immediately after the said bridge should be built'. The Tolls were also fixed: – one shilling for a coach to cross the bridge, sixpence for a cart or wain, and so on down to an halfpenny for each foot passenger, bull, ox or cow. Dike and Cottle were to erect a little house near the bridge for the collector of the tolls. And at their own expense they were to maintain both the bridge and also the stretch of the road from Combe Bridge to Rowas Gate, all this in return for the tolls paid by the users of the Bridge.

The bridge seems to have been completed soon after the signing of the agreement, and certainly before 1739. When Thorpe's map[31] of ' Five Miles round Bath' was published in 1743 it showed 'The New Bridge', with a rather imaginative sketch of what it may have been like. Evidently the road must very soon have become the principal way to Bath. An earlier route was still named on Thorpe's map. This 'Bradford Way to Bath by Warley' followed the present main road from the top of Wine Street in Bradford along what was then known as the Oakway or Oakey Lane, as far as the top of Cottle's Lane. At this point, formerly 'The Hand and Post' or 'The Cross Post', the road turned off along the lane north west through Hartley, past Upper Haugh to Nomansland and then down to Warley, where the river would be crossed. As against 5¾ miles from Bath to the Cross Post by the new bridge, the distance by the old road was 7½ miles, for it involved going round by Bathampton. Then in 1751 the whole road from the Combe Bridge, over the new Stokesford Bridge and on through Winsley to Bradford and beyond was turnpiked by an Act of Parliament, setting up a Bradford Turnpike Trust. It confirmed that George Dike and Moses Cottle junior, sons of the builders, still owned and managed the bridge. But when the Act was renewed in 1776, it says the road ' ... is very hilly, circuitous and much out of repair, and passes over a certain wooden Bridge called Stokes Bridge, which is very narrow, high and dangerous ...'. Apparently, however, no action was taken: it was not rebuilt till after 1783. There are a number of 19th century pictures[32] and photographs of the bridge as it was in that century. Finally there was considerable rebuilding and widening of the bridge in the 1920s.

Of the other roads mapped in 1727 little need be said, for apart from farm tracks, most of them are still with us today. In many places we have seen they clearly cut across parts of the former open fields. Other sections of road are shown as following alongside the strips or their headlands and these may well be surviving parts of older roads. A map of the footpaths in the parish shows a close network of them particularly in the north eastern part. Many will, no doubt, have altered over the years, but one wonders why, for instance, there seem to be seven that converge on a point near the northern exit from the farmyard at Haugh Farm. Was there perhaps once a special reason for meeting at that particular spot? There is a small building nearby – the W.I. scrapbook calls it 'a very old chapel', but it does not now appear to show any sign of being that. Does the meeting point of the paths perhaps indicate that Haugh Farm has itself moved south? The present house is dated 1731, when it was largely rebuilt. It does however contain beams of about 1600 and possibly an old central stack, surviving from an earlier house on its site.

Some Winsley Fields

I N A R U R A L P A R I S H like Winsley, it is natural that much of our knowledge of the early village history comes from the fields and their names. Of course, most of the 350 odd names found in my card index are not of any real interest – names like The Nine Acres for instance. Dozens more look interesting but their meaning is now lost. Only a small selection of these fields can be mentioned here and that selection has to be the author's personal choice.

I would have liked to start with Sheeps Tails, but Avoncliff must come first, for it is probably the oldest name we have.

This name certainly goes back before 1170, for in that year a Shaftesbury Abbey rental introduces us to Nicholaus de Aveneclifa the miller, who had a virgate of land (say about 30 acres hereabouts). Clearly he lived there and, presumably the mill got its name from the riverside meadow where it stood. Going back a bit further, there is good reason for thinking our Avoncliff Mill was one of the two Bradford manorial mills mentioned in the Domesday Book. It looks, too, as if, as well as being around the mill, Avoncliff was a much larger area at some time in the past. It probably stretched right along the hillside – the Cliffe or steep slope above the Avon – at least as far as the bottom of Winsley Hill, perhaps even beyond. But that can only be a conjecture. A clue is that on the 1841 Tithe Map, there still was an 8½ acre field called Avoncliff there.

And so to Sheepstails, a field on the right of the road immediately above the canal bridge as one goes down Winsley Hill. It adds a bit to the village story, for the present field was formed by adding three others, Bushy Leaze, Stubb Leaze, and Muck Leaze to an earlier Sheeps Tails. We know it belonged to John Kent in 1629, but he called it Sheepe Stalls, that is, the shelters where the ewes found shelter at the lambing time. This implies a sizeable flock used to graze on the downs thereabouts. Still well known are two other names, Rowbarrow and Gold Hill. The former is on a projecting bluff above the river west of

Gold Hill. The tramway leads from the bushes on the left is through the trees on the skyline.

Turleigh and the latter nearby, on the west side of Elbow Lane.[33] From the 1727 map, Rowbarrow, named from the Rough Barrow once probably on its most prominent point, may well have been a Furlong of arable strips. The barrow was quarried out in the 19th century to get at the good stone beneath it. It was conveniently close to the tramway which then (the evidence is not quite certain) used to run down the lower part of Elbow Lane to the canal. There is no doubt about the upper part of the tramway; it is still visible crossing Gold Hill diagonally, leading down from The Chase. In 1870s Captain Gibney of Winsley House used to pay a rent of £1 per annum for the use of it in connection with his quarry, sited where The Chase now is.[34] The Rowbarrow earthworks must not be confused with those among the beech trees in the garden at The Chase. Those latter ones are the spoil heaps from Gibney's quarry. Old villagers (no names!) used to suggest that as the quarry infill consolidated itself in the course of the last century, the house would eventually have collapsed into the quarry! As for Gold Hill, neither memories nor records can now tell us whether a rich treasure was dug up there long ago, or if it used to support yet another magnificent crop of buttercups – or could it be named after the Gold Hill at Shaftesbury?

Below these, Bittoms lies on the lower slopes below the hill and like many other so sited fields, probably takes is name from its position. Its upper edge follows the lane from Turleigh via the Elbow bridge over the canal and straight on to 'The Old Weir' across the river. The lane was so marked on the 1727 map and must have been the direct route to Freshford. In the dry summer of 1977 a number of people were able to wade across the river here without difficulty. When the large Bittoms Meadow was divided up, one of its parts became Widow's Bittoms or alternatively Fool's Bittoms or Foots Bittoms (or maybe Foul Bittoms, though I have no record of that) – and who, I wonder, was the widow? And at the same time a long strip of it between the river bank and the railway line beside the aqueduct acquired the curious name of Melancholy Walk – it sound as if it was christened by a 17th or 18th century poet.

We have already come across some field names which perhaps survive from former farms and settlements, now deserted. A fairly recent case of this is France Home Ground near Great Ashley. It was the Home Ground of the vanished France Farm that Thomas Hanks used to farm in 1840[35] and probably takes its name from Sainfoin, a once common fodder crop which used to be known as French Grass.

Mr W. J. Ford, a former County Field Archaeology Officer, identified Edingham and Stamborough as likely to preserve the names of two other deserted sites. Edingham, evidently a Furlong sloping gently up from the Conkwell lane to the top of Knoll Hill, has a name thought to be of Saxon origin – the ham (dwelling) of Edda or Etha's people. Should we suspect a connection here with Edington[36], near the site of King Alfred's victory at Ethandun? As for Stamborough, it lies at a place where the Tithe Map suggests there may have been another Furlong, perhaps once known as Hartley Furlong[37]. 'Stam-' is of course Stane or stone, but 'Borough' could have any one of a number of meanings such as burgh, a defended place, barrow, a burial place, or even berg, a hill, though it would have been a very flat one. It would be rash to choose which is most likely. A neighbouring field, Court's Ground, has nothing to do with manorial courts (or tennis ones for that matter). The name goes back to the 17th century; for in 1674 this field was held by one of Winsley's churchwardens, John A'Court, a member of the A'Court family of Heytesbury Manor.

Then there is Winley. With a name like that, one feels it ought to possible to link it closely to the village itself. There is of course no evidence whatever for thinking that perhaps the village started its existence at Winley, but it remains a mystery, a rather wild guess. The field, bisected by the continuation of Dane Rise Lane leading out to Hartley, was covered with old open field strips on the 1727 map, so it would be unlikely for any signs of an early settlement to survive. Perhaps a careful look at the ground between Winley and Hartley might reveal something, though the land there is much disturbed. The earliest appearance of this name is once again in John Kent's 1629 will.

There are two pieces of land at Winsley by the name of Innox or Innocks, one just west of the village, between the main road and Avonpark, and the other on the west side of Cottles Lane just above the Turleigh houses. Different books give different explanations[38] of the name but in the Middle Ages an Inhook or Inhoke seems to have been a piece of fallow land close to a village, temporarily enclosed, often for a catch crop of peas or beans. This would be done when an increase of cultivated land was needed. Nearly every village has its Innox.

In the north of the parish near Upper Haugh Farm there is a field whose name Many Lands suggests a long history. It may have been a small piece of land left over and made into communal plot when a region of common was being subdivided, its name coming from the Saxon 'gemaene', the community. Then there are Capons and Temple Ground at Oakway, perhaps formed by dividing a single field in two. Capons has nothing to do with ducks. It was parsonage land, so it may be connected with a 16th century John Capon, Bishop of Salisbury, but the name of the field seems to go further back than that. As for Temple Ground, so named in the TA schedule, it would be tempting to think it might once have been owned by the Knights Templar in the middle ages, but in all earlier sources it was called Eastcroft. So, as it is situated so prominently on the hill brow above Belcombe Court, it is more likely to be named after an ornamental temple. Is there perhaps some record say of a Victorian temple near the boundary there?

charter[8] for the grant is generally accepted as genuine and not a forgery, though what we possess is not the original but a 15th century copy in the abbey's Cartulary, their book of charters. It states that the grant was made so as to provide the nuns with a safe refuge from the Danes, as well as a hiding place for the remains of Ethelred's predecessor and half-brother King Edward the Martyr, whose murder had led to the boy Ethelred coming to the throne. As was not uncommon in Saxon charters, this one contains a description, in Old English, of the bounds of the estate. The south and west sections of the boundary are along the River Avon and other streams, and the rest fixed by naming the estates outside the boundary. Across the river from Winsley, there are Westwood, then belonging to the king's huntsman Leofwine[9], Freshford (Ferseforth), and lands of the Abbot of Bath at Midford and Warley. Aelfgar had (Monkton) Farleigh and so on. Clearly all these places were in existence by 1001. What stands out is that none of the places inside the boundary is mentioned, though nearly all the present villages outside are named and therefore already existed. Surely this makes it likely that most of the Bradford villages, inside the boundary, were also there in 1001. And so began the Shaftesbury Era of our history, which was to last till the abbey was dissolved in 1539.

Some eighty six years later, in the Domesday Book, the same story is repeated – once again Winsley and the other Bradford villages are not individually mentioned. This time the silence is because the Domesday Book was drawn up principally to record all the revenue due to the Crown; in the case of Bradford, the whole manor would have paid an annual lump sum to the abbey, there to be included in the abbey's payment to the king. Consequently the amounts due from the individual tithings were not recorded. The Domesday Book does, however, show that by this time a number of small parts of Ethelred's Bradford estate had passed from the abbey to other owners; in particular it states that Ulf – his name is Scandinavian – had acquired one hide of land at Budbury, and now held it directly from the king. We shall see, too, that one of the two Domesday mills at Bradford was in fact Winsley's Avoncliff Mill[10].

Much more is known about Winsley in the next century. Some 12th century pottery sherds have been found in a garden in the centre of the old village[11], perhaps suggesting, though the evidence is far too weak, that this centre did not move far in later years. Much more important are three surveys of the abbey's estates made during that century, in Latin of course, village ('vill') by village. The first two cover almost all the abbey lands in Dorset and Wiltshire, but the third one only Bradford and its villages. What exist now are the fair copies of these surveys, made at some time in the 15th century and entered into the abbey's Cartulary[12] Not surprisingly, the copyists had difficulty in deciphering much of what by then was the 400-year old handwriting of the original documents; and no doubt too the wear and tear over the centuries will have made many parts quite illegible. So a Victorian historian gleefully called the result 'notoriously corrupt', which sounds a bit unfair. It is surely remarkable that the old text should have survived as well as it has. A translation of the Winsley sections is in Appendix 2.

The first survey dates from shortly before the end of Henry I's reign, and probably resulted from trouble about some abbey land at Atworth. It seems that Eulalia[13], who was abbess from 1074 to 1106, had leased several hides of land there to her kinsman Thomas, and Thomas then claimed that the grant was really an outright gift to him. So about 1122 her successor Emma (about 1120 to 1135) had to go to law before the king's court to recover the property. In due course the king's writ[14] went in the abbey's favour and so a few years later, the first survey (technically a rental or custumal) was drawn up to make the position quite clear.

After the chaos of King Stephen's reign, another, more detailed survey was taken about 1170. And again towards the end of the century the third survey followed. This was limited to Bradford and its villages, and was probably taken at a time when the abbess Marie (c.1189 – 1216), King Henry II's sister, was defending the abbey against an attempt by her nephew King Richard I to claim Bradford manor for himself.

For the majority of the abbey's vills, the survey lists all the tenants – at least, we have to assume they were all listed. It records how much land each one held, with the rents and labour services they owed. So here we do at last find out a bit about Winsley. The first survey is not quite complete: the Trowle section is missing, probably included in the borough, and there is no rental for our neighbour, the (Limpley) Stoke tithing, either here or in the later surveys. In this case we can explain what had happened. Instead of the men of Stoke being tenants directly under the Bradford manor in the usual way, their whole tithing had been farmed out to Passat, a prominent Bradford citizen, who paid a yearly rent of 100 s ($£5$) for it, a very large sum in those days. His name appears in the abbess' list of knights who performed the quota of feudal military service demanded by the king from the abbey lands. As well as Stoke, Passat's estate around Bradford was a large one: among others things he had a hide and a half in Tortelee and several houses in the town.[15] Stoke continued to be farmed out in the same way for a long time, for there is an entry in a 13th century document called Nomina Villarum (often named the Testa de Nevill)[16] which records that the farmer then was someone called Hawis Culm.

Most of these village surveys can be identified for they have the known village name as a heading, but a few have lost their names, – particularly in the earliest survey. The problem of identifying two of these presents no difficulty; comparison with lists in later surveys shows they belong to Atworth and Wraxall.

And the remaining anonymous list must be the Winsley one. This is confirmed by its first entry which undoubtedly refers to the same property as the corresponding entry in the second survey. That one, which is named Wineslega, begins with the property of Nicholas de Aveneclifa, the miller. The entry in the first survey may be translated

> GODRIC, 25 shillings for the mill and 15 sticcas of eels and 1 acre of ploughing (labour) and 1 of fallowing; and he reaps 1 acre in August, and he lends his wagon for 1 day (weekly?, or at harvest?), and every year he shall have one beam from the woods for repairing the mill with the help of men and carts (from the village), and for fetching (new) millstones.

There was often a connection between mills and eels in the 12th century, because in those days mill weirs were ideal fishing enclosures. A sticca was a large basket, big enough to hold 25 fully grown eels, which no doubt would have to be sent to Shaftesbury, a special treat for the nuns. Godric's duty of fallowing meant a light ploughing of fallow land, just enough to keep the weeds down.

Only in the 1170 survey do we at last find a village list with the Latin heading 'Wineslega', and the entry heading this list is very similar to Godric's. In that year and in 1190 Godric's successor was Nicholas de Aveneclifa. He, like Godric, had to provide 15 sticcas of eels, so clearly all three lists refer to the same mill at Avoncliff on the Winsley bank of the river, for, remember, the Westwood bank did not belong to the abbey [17]. The cash rent had gone down to 20 shillings, and the miller had an extra virgate of land – say 25 acres – [or perhaps that was one of the 'notorious corruptions' that they merely miscopied at some stage!]. By the 1190s, too, the villagers no longer had to help with the new millstones – Nicholas had to organise it himself. He was also involved in organising the two annual Scot Ales (Scotalium in the Latin!). Attendance at these events was compulsory; they were fund raisers for church upkeep, one 'for the Lady', i.e. the Abbess, and the other for the local (Bradford) church. Each household had to pay a 3½ pence entrance fee. Each of the three surveys also records the mill in the town, which had to provide 25 sticcas a year. It is interesting that by 1170 the miller at Bradford was Walter de Aula, the earliest known member of the well known Hall family at Bradford, unless of course his predecessor Richard in 1132 was an even earlier Hall.

This 1170 survey, though it contains the earliest known written mention of Winsley, also contains a note referring us back before 1132 to Winsley in the time of Cecilia, who was Abbess of Shaftesbury probably from 1107 to 1120. The note states that she gave half a hide at Winsley for the support of Bradford church, plus a quarter of a virgate, perhaps for keeping the altar lamps burning [18]. Her gift would amount to sixty or seventy acres altogether, and may well have been the start of what over the centuries was to develop into the Prebendal or Rectorial Manor of Bradford. One guesses that the land was more or less the same as the sixty acres or so said to belong to the Parsonage Farm in a Parliamentary survey[19] in 1649. The age of this farm is indicated by the presence next to the farmhouse of a field called the Conyger, a name that as we have seen would only be given to a field in the earliest days of rabbit farming. This may mean that soon after 1100 the cultivated land at Winsley had already spread beyond the village's common fields, out to the Parsonage Farm and beyond. Here then is another pointer to Winsley's probable existence well before that century.

Each of these Shaftesbury surveys contains lists of those who held land at each of the abbey's 'vills', i.e. hamlets, villages and towns. Thirty-two households are named at Winsley in 1132, twenty eight in 1170 and thirty three at the end of the century. Evidently Winsley was one of the more populous tithings round Bradford in the 12th century; for instance, by comparison with the Winsley tithing's 30 odd houses, there were only 41 named house owners in the borough. (It does however seem that many of the more prosperous burghers each owned several houses). There were 17 households in the Atworth tithing, 15 at Wraxall and about thirty at Holt, which then included Leigh and Woolley. These figures may suggest that Winsley had an overall population of round about a hundred and fifty in those days, more if there were landless labourers here as well. The small changes in the number of holdings from survey to survey could well occur in the natural course of events, for instance if a father left two sons who split the family holding between them. And between the first two surveys lay King Stephen's reign, with his unsuccessful siege of Trowbridge castle in 1139. Most inhabitants of Winsley had Saxon names in 1132, but Norman ones were becoming commoner later in the century.

The holdings in Bradford's vills naturally varied considerably in size, so each would have its own distinctive pattern of large and small farms. For instance in Winsley in 1170, there were two large farms each of 1 hide, (say normally around 120 acres, or 50 hectares – it was not a fixed size), two more of half a hide, three of 1½ virgates (20 or 30 acres) and 23 of 1 virgate or less. And Wigant had a mere 2½ acres, for which he did two days labour each week on the manor land. Could he, one wonders, grow enough on that small patch for his family to live on? This village pattern remained essentially the same in all three surveys, the main changes being, say, when two half virgate holdings were joined into one whole virgate. Wraxall was very similar, but Atworth was a village with two very large holdings, a hide and a half each, and only seven small farms. One of the large ones had been Thomas' estate, and there were signs that it was being treated like a sub-manor, managing much of its own affairs. Most of the 1-virgate farms had the right to graze a stated number of animals on the common meadow, but they paid a wide diversity of rents. Thus at Winsley, Ulsi had one virgate for which he 'owes (a cash rent of) 15 pence yearly and every week he must provide half a wagon[20] and half a horse and do labour every day' on the manor fields (the 'demesne'); he also owed an amber of flour (the annual Chirisset, another church tax). Wiclac, another 1-virgate holder, paid a 5s cash rent and an amber of flour, but by contrast, did not have any labour duties to do. Others had duties like ploughing two acres of the demesne land in winter, fallowing them in summer and reaping them at the harvest. Many of these differences would correspond to varying needs of the manor as a whole, but these examples perhaps suggest that as time went by, cash rents were becoming commoner, replacing some of the labour services. By 1132 rents and labour duties like these must already have remained steady long enough for such changes in their organisation to have happened.

One of the two 1-hide farms at Winsley was the hide at Budbury held by Ulf in the Domesday Book. The Abbess Emma bought it from Ulf's successor Saccon and his sons. As tenants of the abbey, they owed Suit of Court, that is allegiance, at the County and Hundred Courts. The other hide we cannot locate – was it perhaps the main farm at Turleigh, or what we now know as the Manor Farm? Held by Hunelanus in 1132, it owed the same suits of court, but its rent was only 10s; he or his men had to plough two acres of demesne land in winter and fallow them in summer. In the third survey the two owners were William of Budbury and Magister (Master) Ham. They evidently held some kind of official positions at the county Sheriff's Court, attending there when it was their turn of duty. They were also in charge of organising the local Scot Ales.

Several of those who held half a hide of land appear to have had additional manorial work to do, supplying a plough (and team) as well as a horse for carriage duty. They had daily work to do on the manor land, and had to give two ambers of flour.

The rest of the tenants had smaller holdings, say half a virgate each. These fifteen labourers made up half the village's population; the survey gives little information about them. There was a widow among them, no doubt allowed to retain her late husband's land 'according to the Customs of the Manor' – a custom described in the survey, and still quoted in manor court rolls until the 17th or even 18th centuries. Two of these men paid a small cash rent; for the rest there is a standard formula:- So and So 'for his half virgate does four days labour each week and owes four hens for Chirisset'. Could it really mean that all these 60 odd hens, with corresponding numbers from the other villages, all arrived on the Bradford priest's doorstep on a particular day of the year?... And did some of those hens have to be taken to Shaftesbury?

The communal work was managed, like much else in Winsley, by the village Bedel. In 1132 he was Ulfric, who was a villager himself. He had a one-virgate holding of his own, and his bedelry work earned him an extra virgate of land, which he would have to pass on to his successor when his term of office ended. Bradford manor as a whole was organised from Barton Farm; in the later middle ages at least the Barton Farm may well have been in Trowle, for the staff lived in that tithing. Alas, the Trowle part of the 1132 survey is missing, leaving us in the dark about the set up at that time.

A curious feature of the 1132 survey is that as well as lists for such familiar neighbours as Wraxall, Atworth and Holt, there was Tortelega[21], a small place with only seven households. It is tempting, of course, to follow many writers who have assumed this name must be an early disguise for Turleigh, and others who suggest that possibly Tortelega is now Trowle. But one's suspicions are roused by the first abbey survey where Torteleg' seems associated with Holt rather than Winsley. Later, there is a deed of 1418[22] dealing with the conveyance of several messuages, one of them at Throu(n)tlegh and another at Turleigh. Surely therefore, these two places must be different. To try to answer the question, let us take a closer look at the list of holdings at Torteleg' – in particular at what seems to have happened to the very distinctive holding which Ailward, the chief landholder, held in 1132. Like Passat, he had half a hide and was one of the Abbess' knights in the king's service. He was the only Bradford man who owed what may be called 'errand-service' at his own expense 'on this side of the sea' and at the abbess' expense 'on the other side of the sea'. Did he perhaps have to travel to Normandy? Moving on to the next survey, there is no mention of Torteleg', but at Holt, Nicholaus de Hastun for his half hide owed what I imagine to be a shortened version of the same errand-service. It looks as if by 1170 Tortelegh had been absorbed into Holt,[23] suggesting that it may have been near there. Then in the third survey at the end of the century the situation seems clearer. The bounds of Holt had changed again; Woolley (now including the Tortelegh lands and probably Bradford Leigh as well) had been split off again from Holt, to make a new 'vill' called Woolley, – they wrote Wlfleg' (i.e. Ulf's Legh) or Wollewelle – with its own tenants' list. The exact location of Tortelegh remains uncertain. By the fourteenth century the name Tortelegh' appears as Thorntelegh – and sometimes they even wrote it Phromtelegh! Thorntelegh seems to have passed into either Hall's Manor or Rogers' Manor at Bradford, the latter, with its known land near Woolley and Holt, being the more likely. Later on, it is just possible that the name Thorntelegh gradually changed via Phrontelegh and Francelegh[24] into Frankley!

There seem to have been few changes at Winsley in the years leading up to the second survey, that is, about half way through the reign of Henry II. Nicholas of Aveneclifa was then the miller there and Radus (short for Radulphus or Ralph) the village Bedel. Of the four men acting as jurors who collected the material for the survey, one was Alfric Munnuc. Munnuc being the Saxon word for a monk, he would perhaps have been chosen for the task because he could write and read. He was also called Alfric of the Well – was that Lady Well in Newtown? It is almost certain that there was no church or chapel in Winsley village in 1170 but Ladywell, then in Winsley tithing, is reasonably near Bradford church or, if it existed in the 12th century, to the Hermitage on Tory. Either way, Ladywell would be a likely place to find a monk. Alfric had to pay the same 4s rent as many other 1-virgate men. As well as ploughing, fallowing and reaping one acre of the demesne land, he was required to do carriage duty, which probably involved driving his wagon as far as Shaftesbury before the feasts at Christmas and Easter. And he had to carry messages for the Lady Abbess as she required.

Several of the hamlets around Winsley are first mentioned in this survey; we read of the land of Reginald de Aslega ('of Ashley'), who had half a virgate there, and Radus de Ag' (Haugh) who had a hide, a large holding for those days. On the other hand we still seem to have no reliable trace of Turleigh.

Several of the men named in 1170 were still around when the third survey was made in the 1190s. In this, it looks as if a number of the questions the jurors were asked to answer were new ones. Thus three Winsley men, Nicholas the Avoncliff miller, with Magister Ham and William de Buddebere (Budbury) were to go to – maybe that means 'to go and organise' – the two annual Scot Ales as we saw earlier. And by then there were three 'monks' with land in Winsley, Athelinus monachus, who was Alfric's successor, Willelmus (William) monachus who had only half a virgate, doing labouring work four days a week (increasing to every day at Harvest) and receiving a labourer's allowance of grain on Thursdays, and Radus monachus who had even less land.

The duties owed to the abbey by Athelinus differ from his predecessor Alvric's mainly in his having to find a man and half a wagon for the haymaking at Yeamead and Muchelmead, which are meadows by the Avon out towards Staverton. They also and do some work at the vineyard. This last duty raises numerous questions. A vineyard at Bradford is first mentioned in the Domesday Book. It says there was 'one arpent of vineyard' – I wonder how large that was. The book gives no hint of its whereabouts: it could be anywhere in the whole Bradford estate. After that there is then no mention of a vineyard till the 1170 survey in which two men, Reginald of Leigh and Godfrid of Brocheshilla (i.e. Wraxall), each had to send a man for a day's work 'ad vineam'. This could mean 'at the vineyard' or 'at the grape harvest'. Was this perhaps the old vineyard still flourishing, or a new one being created? Twenty years later, in the last survey, a much larger workforce was needed – 8 men from Winsley, 3 from Trowle and 4 from Holt. There is also the confusing statement that four Wraxall men had to work there too, but that seems to contradict the statement that 'all the men at Wrokesham except for the free tenants must find a man for 2 days work at the vineyard'. Perhaps we should deduce that in 1170 the vineyard was at Wraxall.

Some notes in the 1190 survey show another side of the running of the village at the end of the twelfth century. We noted that each village's affairs were in the hands of a Bedel who was a local man, and that in 1132 Ulfric, the Bedel at Winsley had, besides his own farm, another virgate of land 'for his Bedelry'. One would like to know what he had to do to earn this. His successor in 1170 had a farm of half a hide. As well as the usual ploughing etc. he did carriage service in preparation for the feasts at Christmas and Easter, perhaps going as far as Shaftesbury. The last survey tells of another side of the job.

> The Bedel shall have one acre of corn for his pay and for Budelstich[25] and one sedlep (a basket in which seed was carried by the sower) of wheat before Christmas and one sedlep of oats before Easter because he must manage the village sowing after the ploughing. He shall have one deisef (perhaps a dish of grain) each day from the start of the Harvest till the whole has been gathered in, and from then on he must set a watch day and night and must make good without loss double if any be stolen or damaged by pack horses.

On the other hand, during the haymaking, it was decreed that: 'All those who mow and spread the hay in the meadow shall have 15 pence (between them?) and two sheep when the task is finished.' And: 'At the Laqueritia (whatever that was) all those who provide and maintain a wagon shall receive their food, or three pence.'

The men of the village seem to have been quit of tolls on all they bought and sold on market days at Bradford, except on live horses and mules. And at the annual Holy Trinity Fair in May, they were also free of tolls for as long as the fair should last. This Trinity Fair continued to be held annually till well into the 19th century on common land at Bradford Leigh.

The more capable men of the village also had to perform various tasks outside the Bradford area.[26] Two of them had regular duties as messengers – very important in a semi literate society. Others had to attend the Hundred and County Sheriff's courts where they 'owed Suit of Court'. And evidently the carriage duties at Christmas and Easter involved quite a convoy of carts and pack horses making the journey to the abbey. Nobody at Winsley, however, was charged a responsible duty as like that of Walter de Stone of Bradford. We read that 'He must go at the Lady's expense between four manors (the survey actually says four 'maria', i.e. seas! [27]) ... and lead one nun by (her horse's) reins and carry her saddle bags on foot (because his ancestors did not have a horse) as far as Gloucester'.

3
The Later Middle Ages

THE TWELFTH CENTURY SURVEYS, with their plentiful details of hides, virgates, and services owed by the farmers in their large or smaller holdings, leave one wondering what sort of life the people of Winsley lived in those days. Even less is known about the local picture in the period that followed and what we do know is less sharply drawn. We have, for instance, a few Winsley court cases recorded from the Wiltshire Eyre of 1249[1]. The court dealt with a case of murder that year, the victim being a certain William de Wynsele, slain in the common field at Biddestone. We can only ask what a Winsley man was doing so far from his home village – was he maybe up to no good there, or perhaps a merchant carrying a valuable stock in trade, – or just visiting his aunt? More likely, his name simply implies that he or his family had come from Winsley and were living at Biddestone.

In the same year there was also the sad case of a boy named David, who was found torn to pieces under the water wheel of Avenecliff mill – not the first such accident, one fears, and certainly not the last. The clerk of the court recorded that 'The first finder, Maud his mother, does not come 'to the court' so she was attached by Everard de la Hacche of Aveneclive and William the miller of the same. So they are in mercy. No one is suspected: so misadventure. Price of the wheel is 13d.' Evidently the mill wheel was to be punished, as the real murderer! The owner of the mill wheel would have to pay the court this 'deodand' [2].

On a more cheerful note is the case of Robert Wayfer – could he be our earliest known weaver? Probably not;; the name Webbe was the usual one for a weaver in those centuries. Wayfer brought a case before the court, claiming that he was being denied certain rights customarily belonging to his free-holding at Winsley. These rights were for a certain number of his cattle to graze at a named place in Selwood. The Forest records imply that at this period Selwood Forest stretched as far north as the river Avon; in any case such grazing rights were often on waste land and at a considerable distance away from the holder's own farm. For some reason, Wayfer and his sponsors seem to have abandoned their plea. So the court fined them for not appearing there on the stated day. These three cases are all taken from the year 1249, that being the only one for which the Court Pleas have been printed. The Wiltshire Record Society is however expected to publish the pleas for 1268 shortly.

At some time in this period, the earliest Winsley church must have been built. According to the first of the three Shaftesbury surveys, one Edwin was the priest at Bradford church in 1132. He was in fact in charge of three churches, the other two being at Atworth and at Stoke (i.e. Limpley Stoke, another church with Saxon features)[3]. The survey makes no mention of a church or chapel at any other of the Bradford villages. In the later surveys, we did however see there were some men at Winsley with the title 'monachus', the monk, men who may have provided some pastoral care in the village.

It is not until much later, in 1349, that we do find a definite written record of churches in any more of the Bradford villages. This comes in a decree sent to the Abbess of Shaftesbury from Robert Wyvil, then bishop of Salisbury[4]. Over a long period, negotiations had been slowly grinding on in connection with the abbey's request for permission to impropriate[5] the church at Bradford, that is, to convert its rectory into a vicarage (yes, there was a difference!). It would have involved the exchange of a series of documents, requesting and being granted 'licences to impropriate' between the successive abbesses, and bishops, not to mention the Archbishop of Canterbury, the King, the Pope and no doubt others. Sometime in this period, in 1291, a decree[6] from Pope Nicholas I, levying a tax, tantalisingly mentions 'The Church of Bradeforde with its Chapels' – but, of course, without naming these chapels. Was Winsley one? Bishop Wyvil's indenture, at the end of the process, laid down the final details of the scheme. It contains the vital phrases 'We will and ordain that the vicar (of Bradford) aforesaid and his successors have and shall have all the oblations and small tithes[7] of the Town of Bradford .... Also the Tythes of Wool and all oblations and small tithes coming to the chapels of Wynesleye and Holte '. Similar arrangements were also set up for the chapels of Wroxhale, Ateworth and Stoke. It would seem likely that about this time the church land was reorganised into a 'Prebendal' manor, a sub manor of the main Bradford manor. The only early trace of this is that in the main manor accounts[14] for the 22nd year of the Abbess Joan Formage (1374) there survives a small portion of the account telling of the wheat and oats delivered by the 'Personatus', the Parsonage manor, often later called the Rectory.

That old Winsley church was demolished in 1841, but many details of its appearance can be seen in the watercolour painted in 1808 by J.Buckler[8], an artist well known for the accuracy of his work. Our church is shown, with a background of open country. This confirms the picture's date, for a few years

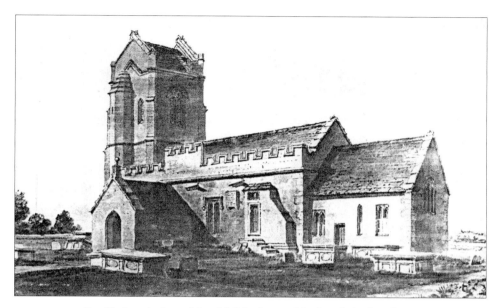

Buckler's painting of the old Winsley parish church in the 1800s.

later, by 1816, a row of cottages, now nos. 147 -149 Winsley, would probably have appeared west of the church. The picture shows it was a small church, too narrow to have had aisles, but with quite a large porch. Its small chancel was slightly narrower than the nave. The eaves of the nave were battlemented and the nave itself probably of ashlar. Most of the windows are square headed, with two lights, a form common over a long period, particularly in the 15th century. The lights may have had cinquefoil cusps at their heads but it is difficult to be sure of this from the picture. Those on the nave look somewhat later in date than the chancel ones, suggesting alterations, perhaps even a partial rebuild, made to the nave in the 15th century or later. The date of the stonework of the chancel looks earlier than that of the nave. And as well as two square headed chancel windows, the picture shows a tall, narrow lancet window there. This would mean the chancel was built say around the mid-13th century – perhaps before 1250, with its other windows added later. The east end of the chancel is painted in rather deep shadow, so it is hard to see what the east window was like. It is, however probable that it had a triplet of lancets, the central one a bit taller than the outer ones, and the whole under a hood mould (the figure shows a window of this type in another church). This again suggests a mid-13th century date for the chancel.

The church tower narrowly escaped demolition with the rest of the old church in 1841. Like the old nave, it is 15th century work. It has changed little since Buckler's picture, but the clock, said to have been put in place in the eighteenth century, is not shown in the picture, nor are the gargoyles or masks high up on the tower's east and west faces.

Over most of England the twelfth century had been a time of considerable population growth, and a period of warmer climate had favoured the expansion of the cultivated land to feed the extra mouths. By the end of the thirteenth century, though, the increases in food production possible with the farming methods of those days were reaching their limits. In some places, like those near to expanses of moorland, waste land outside the village fields could be brought into cultivation, but such land tended to be of poor quality. Growing family sizes also led to subdivision of farms into smaller and smaller units, with over-cultivation of the fields leading to further reduced crops. On the other hand, documents survive to show how efforts were being made at a number of Wiltshire villages from the 14th century onwards to increase the yield from the land by changing from a two field system of cultivation to a three or even four field rotation

A typical triple lancet window of c.1230. Buckler' painting suggests that the old parish church chancel was slightly later than this.

under which a smaller proportion of the land was left fallow each year[9] and so more could be cultivated.

On top of this several new factors appeared to make life harder. In the years after 1300 the climate grew cooler. Not surprisingly, famines became more frequent. Then came the disaster of the previously unknown Great Plague, the one now usually called the Black Death, spreading rapidly and repeatedly after its arrival in 1348.

All this was the general picture. Whether and to what extent it was true for the Bradford region and for Winsley in particular is very unsure. For a start there is the question of the growth of the population. We have already seen that at the end of the 12th century there were 33 households in the village. Then in 1327, at the beginning of the reign of King Edward III[10] there is a list of those paying a tax or 'subsidy' called 'Fifteenths and Tenths', and it names only 20 households. There were probably more, because all those who had less than a certain amount of 'movable goods' – all the cottagers and smaller tradesmen for instance, – were exempted from payment. The same tax was levied again in 1332 [11] This time there were 36 names, an apparent increase of 80% in only five years! That needs a bit of explaining away, and we can only guess at the real cause – was there, for instance, tax dodging on a massive

scattered round Westbury and Bratton as well as out to Southwick and beyond. Not content with this, Mareys, after the death of John de Edyngdon in 1387, at last obtained the manor of Pombury, and then brought the manor of Whaddon into his empire. Finally, in 1393, an entry in the Edington Cartulary[23] reveals what we should have guessed all along. It records a letter from Joan Formage, the Abbess of Shaftesbury and her attorney John Mareys, bailiff of Bradford, putting the rector and brethren of Edington Priory in possession of the advowson of Keevil. So it was as a lawyer that Mareys had his fingers in all those land deals, as well as being high enough up the tree at Bradford to be given the office of bailiff. And then he disappears from the scene. As usual in the middle ages, none of these deeds gives any real clue to whereabouts in Winsley his property lay. And in the deeds of those days, the numbers of messuages and the rest are likely to be considerably exaggerated.

We turn now to John Aysshele, who was assessed for 6s.8d, Winsley's largest poll tax payment. He belonged to a family who had lived in Winsley – at Ashley, in fact – for several centuries. Every so often, the name (de) Ashley or a variant of that spelling occurs in some document, and in the absence of other evidence, we may suppose they belonged to the same family. The story begins with Reginald de Aslega, tenant of half a virgate of land, a small clearing in the village waste land, for which he paid a rent of 15d. a year and had to reap half an acre of the manorial land, according to the 1170 Shaftesbury survey. He was followed by Walter de Haslega, probably his son, in the third survey[24]. There follows a silent interval till Roger de Asselegh was a tenant of Bradford manor in 1280; then in both the 1327 and 1332 subsidies John de Ayssheleye comes second in the Winsley list. It looks as if they had expanded their farm quite a bit in the interval. And in the 1377 it was another John, presumably his son or grandson, who paid that large sum. By then their property had spread beyond Winsley, for in 1356 Reynold (that is Reginald) was party to a conveyance – a so called 'Feet of Fine' – of a third part of 2 messuages, 2 mills and so on at Overwestwode, Netherwestwode (Upper and Lower Westwood) and Avoncliff. These mills would be on the Westwood side of the river at Avoncliff. The property went to William de Iforde. Sometime soon after this, they added Budbury to their property at Ashley; it came to be called the manor of Ashley and Budbury and so it was in a court book of Bradford manor early in Henry VIIth's reign. However at some time in the reign of Henry VI a branch of the family had begun to move away from Ashley. Robert Ashley married Gill (Egidia), daughter and heir of Sir John Hauskyn (died 1476), and so acquired the important manor of Wimborne St Giles in Dorset. Ashley, of course, remained family property, for Hugh (died 1493) held the manor of 'Ashle beside Bradford'. It is not clear just when it became the 'manor of Ashley and Budbury', a sub-manor of Bradford.

There was little change for nearly the next century, but then in 1578 the Winsley link was broken. A deed survives, in which Sir Henry Ashley of Wimborne St Giles, Dame Catharine his wife, his son and heir Henry Ashley Esq. and Sir Henry's brother Anthony, conveyed all their property at Ashley and Budbury to John Blanchard of Marshfield for £620.[25] After this, there does not seem to have been any further connection between the family and our village and its neighbourhood or with the hamlet of Ashley. The Anthony Ashley above, later Sir Anthony, became clerk to the Privy Council. He married Dorothy Lyte of Lytes Cary in Somerset, and their daughter Ann (died 1628) married Sir John Cooper and their son Anthony Ashley-Cooper was created the first Earl of Shaftesbury – and the 7th Earl was the eminent politician and friend of the poor.

In the years before the dissolution of the Abbey, some of the manor court minute records for Bradford have been preserved, with entries about Winsley. There are a few from the start of the reign of Henry VII [26], and a thick court book covering nearly all the abbey's estates in 1517 and 1518 [27]. The business of the court was on the whole very routine, recording grants of land holdings, often after the death of the previous tenant. Even so, though, one reads of the Winsley property of well known men such as Thomas Horton. A prosperous clothier, his memoral brass in Bradford church displays his merchant's mark prominently, the mark he would have attached to his bales of cloth. The founder of a chantry in that church in 1524, he went on to build the old Church Hall and then a fine house for himself; it stands behind Abbey House. The messuage and a farundell[28] of land he held at Winsley in 1488 seems a small matter compared with his manors at Westwood and Iford.

In the 1517 court book there is the usual list of fines for non attendance at the Bradford court, mostly from absentee landlords such as Sir Edward Hungerford of Farleigh Castle and Sir John Lisle. But Henry Ashley was 'essoined', spared the fine as he had sent his apology for absence. Four others, lesser folk, got fines of a few pence. They had been reported at the previous court because their houses in Winsley were in a state of disrepair – they were quite literally 'decasus' – falling down. Furthermore there was a threat of further massive fines, 6s.8d each, if the repairs were not satisfactorily completed before the Court next met.

Two of these offenders, Joan Wylshyre, a widow, and her son Thomas, a tailor, living in Turleigh were in trouble in another serious way. They were evidently caught up in a campaign the bishop of Salisbury was pursuing against Lollardy. The bishop's Register[29] contains the confessions (abjurations) extracted from nearly forty of these 'hereticks', among them Joan and Thomas Wylshyre. It must have been a frightening experience for these people, small tradesmen, to come up before the Archdeacon at the Bishop's court at Ramsbury for cross questioning on their beliefs. Joan and Thomas each abjured their Lollardy in what looks like a standard wording – that they had kept company many times with 'certen mysbelvynge persons and heretiks', who 'held and tawght certen false opynyons'. The main stress was laid on believing that 'it is lawfull .... to ete flesh in yᵉ lente tyme' and on other fasting days. Their condemnation follows in latin, the gist of which seems to be that they were to make a public renunciation of these things three times, in the parish church at Bradford on the 8th of August next (1518), in the chapel at Winsley on the following Sunday and in the church at Trowbridge on August 23rd. At each place they would process round with feet, legs and head bare, carrying bundles of wooden faggots on their shoulders, proclaiming their penitence in a clear voice.

Another Wylshyre, Henry, also a Turleigh weaver, was probably a leading light in the group. He was accused in addition of denying the doctrine of transubstantiation and the worship of images. He was condemned to process round the market place at Bradford proclaiming his guilt from ten o'clock till eleven amid the derision of a large mocking mob which was to be organised by the curate, and all this was to be repeated a week later at Trowbridge.[30]

Early Houses

I T IS DURING this late medieval period that we begin to be able to identify a few houses around Winsley still containing some traces of what they may formerly have been. The present chapter looks at their early history; we will take up the rest of their stories in later pages. Most houses built in the later middle ages would have had timber framed walls rather than stone ones, but in Winsley very little trace of such construction has survived, even in the shape of old timbers built into their stone successors. What does remain of such early stone walls is often a more or less formless piece of rubble wall now incorporated in a younger wall, with very little to distinguish the small rubble stone work dating from one such early period from that of the rest of the wall. As a general rule, a good tentative assumption is that the thicker the rubble wall, the older it is likely to be, other things being equal. The quality of the stone, the social status of the building and its probable use come into the picture too. Pamela Slocombe, in her most helpful books[31] for the Wiltshire Buildings Record, states that with the best quality limestone from around Corsham, Box and Bradford it has been found that sections of wall from the 16th century usually are about 26 in. (66 cm.) thick, diminishing to 24 in. (60 cm) in the early 17th and to 22 in. in the 18th century. Earlier walls are often considerably thicker but are more variable, making comparable figures less accurate. Old timber roofs, on the other hand, are in some ways more likely to survive over longer periods and can be studied from the details of their carpentry.

(left) Parsonage Farm seen from the east.

(below) Parsonage Farm, front view with the medieval block on the left.

The house descriptions that follow are largely to be found in inspection reports by the authors, deposited with the Wiltshire Buildings Record.

We have seen that since the beginning of the 12th century Shaftesbury Abbey has had a demesne farm at Haugh. Probably therefore this monastic 'grange' would soon have acquired a farmhouse, and Parsonage Farm, the house standing there today, has sections of old walls in one or two places which seem to belong well back to these earliest years. It faces east and consists basically of a single range of rooms. At the south end there is a rather tower like building, three storeys high. The part to the north is lower, much of it built in the latter part of the 16th century. The ground floor of the tower block has some much thicker walls except in its south wall, which has clearly been rebuilt. The thickness of the west wall is mostly 38' (96 cm.) and the east 36' (90 cm.). At the north end, where it joins the later range, there is a 33' (84 cm.) wall, suggesting that it too was once an exterior wall. This is not all. On the east, where the two parts of the house join, the front door leads in from the porch through a 12 foot length of wall that is even thicker – 42' (107 cm.). All this massive masonry must have been put up very early when it was a high class monastic building. Perhaps we can interpret the wall fragment by the porch as the earliest survivor, built well before the bottom of the south tower, which itself comes from sometime between the 14th and the start of the 16th centuries. But what it would have looked like at these various stages of its development we cannot tell.

The Manor House is another of the very early houses whose date can be estimated from measurements of the wall thicknesses. It was probably the

Old sketch of the manor.

Shaftesbury Abbey's demesne farm from an early date, undergoing a number of major or partial rebuildings over the years. Apart from the early 20th century block at the west end, the main section of the present house is an east-west range, most of whose outside walls are 30' (76 cm.) or in a few places 32' (81 cm.) thick. The house is now divided into two halves, possibly with a cross passage between. This part of the house could well have been built shortly before the date 1612 on a stone above a blocked door between the halves bearing the initials IMK for John (1558 – 1630) and Mary Kent. A curious wing running roughly south east projects from the south east corner with walls 34 or 35' (86 or 89 cm.)' thick. This wing, one room long, is at an angle of 15° more than a right angle to the main house. One guesses that it was older than the rest. – say the 15th century or early 16th. By the way, a local stonemason, the late Phil Beaven, apparently claimed to have moved that date stone into its present position from somewhere else in the house.

Nearby stands the Manor Farm, as it is now called, much of it a rather earlier building. We guess that this was in the occupation of John Hendy or John Withie around 1600. It contains a Hall and Parlour in a one or one and a half storeyed house. In the north end wall of the Hall, formerly the exterior north wall of the house, is a massive stone chimney stack with an impressive

Manor Farm , as it was (left) and is (right).

fireplace in the Hall. It must go back to the 15th century. The old photograph confirms that the house was thatched until fairly recently. And attached to the north end is a high, two and a half storey 18th century building with a Mansard roof and heavy timbers, implying that heavy goods were stored there – weaving or grain storage suggest themselves for its purpose. Nearly all the exterior walls of the hall and parlour are 36 to 38 ins (90 – 95 cm.) thick. The farm fields of the Manor, itself a major farm, are quite distinct from those of this 'Manor Farm'. There seems to be no link between the two. Is 'Manor Farm' a recent name?

A set of clues of a different kind are all we have for searching out the early growth of Burghope, the old house at the western end of the village. The middle part of its main range is clearly of a considerable age, most of the rest being added in the 19th century or later. Unfortunately the house's deeds do not seem to go back beyond the mid seventeenth century. However the earliest part of the house was originally a two bay hall, open to the roof and undoubtedly often full of smoke. The truss between the two bays was particularly blackened by the open fire under it. It is of an unusual design, without parallel in the country, and a recent study by dendrochronology[32] reveals that it was made from a tree felled in the summer of 1317. The unusual truss form suggests that there may have been a smoke louvre here in the days before chimneys came into use in village houses and in the late 15th century a very handsome stone fireplace was built against the south wall, an upper floor was inserted and the space on each floor was divided into two rooms. In one corner of the fireplace

Burghope. The oldest part is in the middle – and that replaces a much older house.

an inscription, still just legible, reads 'Remember the Sabbath'. This is reputed to be taken from Cranmer's version, the Great Bible of 1540, and the room was therefore called the Cranmer Room.

We do not know if the walls of this early hall were of stone or timber, but it would be possible to estimate its date roughly if its roof, reputedly a very fine structure, were more easily accessible. However during building work in the late 19th century a curious leather-bound wooden shield was found, buried in one of the walls. This was purchased by the British Museum in 1886 from John Broad of Dane Villa, and was for many years displayed on loan in the Tower Armouries at the Tower of London. These Armouries have recently been re-housed at Leeds and one presumes that our shield now resides there. A copy of a letter from the Keeper of Armour will be found in the notes[33]. It will be seen that the Keeper 'tentatively dated the Winsley buckler to the 15th century, but there is no real reason for excluding a date in the 14th century or perhaps even the early 16th century. The

The late medieval Winsley Shield, found hidden in an old wall at Burghope.

Winsley buckler is a very rare piece and comparison is virtually impossible'. It is plausible to expect the same range of date to apply to the old part of the house also.

Burghope has, unfortunately, been the victim of Canon Jones' initial confusion between Winterslow (Wintresleu) which was in the Domesday Book and Winsley which was not. He later corrected this opinion, not before it was immovably fixed in the local folklore. Here it has led to the statement in the W.I.Scrapbook that the Burghope fireplace was erected by a member of the Benstede family, who, it says, occupied the house for nearly 200 years. What they actually occupied was not Winsley but the manor of West Winterslow.[34] This error is probably also the reason why it was often claimed that Burghope was 'The Manor of Olden Times'. That cannot be correct. Winsley, and Burghope in particular, has its fair share of tales of subterranean passages. Why or when so much effort should have been spent in tunnelling from a cellar at Burghope to Winsley Manor is never explained. The tale of a similar, surely ridiculous and fictitious, passageway leading west from Scarth could have been suggested by the cellar there.

Another building which probably dates back to the 15th century is The Lyns, a very interesting house in the middle of Turleigh. Facing east onto the road at

The Lyns, Turleigh, abutting on to Green Lane (left), with detail of 16th century ceiling beams in the hall (right).

the junction of Green Lane, it has a 'hall and crosswing' plan, a type which was commonly used throughout the 15th and well into the 16th century. The cross wing runs east to west at the upper end of the hall; it appears to have been two storeyed from the start, with parlour below and chamber above. The hall was originally open to the roof, as evidenced by the smoke blackening there. To the south of the hall was a cross passage running east – west; and south of that in what was literally the 'lower end' of the house was a service room. The rubble walls of the cross wing, including that separating it from the hall, vary between 29 and 32 ins. thick, suggesting that it formed the original house to which a timber framed hall was added, a combination met elsewhere in the county. There is a blocked doorway in the front wall on the first floor over the hall; perhaps this room was at one time used for storage of heavy goods, raised up by a hoist. The walls at the back of the main range are 26' thick, so it was not so old as the cross wing. On the front, however the stonework is different and the window mullions are of the small ogee type used in the later 18th century. This suggests a re-facing of the front; that is confirmed from inside, for here the tops of the windows of the south rooms rise well above the ceilings.

The roof has its original trusses; they are smoke blackened and of steep pitch, so the first roof would have been thatched. Both the hall and wing roofs are blackened, and the rooms would not initially have had stacks. The hall roof has evidence of wind braces, pairs of curved beams in the slope of the roof, which were ornamental as well as having their structural function. The nature of the roof, and the details of the wing suggest that the house was first built at the end of the 15th century. The first major change to the house was the rebuilding of the timber walls of the hall in stone and the insertion of a large

The Croft, a fifteenth century house.

stack there, backing as usual on to the cross passage. Once a chimney was available, it was no longer necessary to have such a high room to deal with the smoke problem, so a first floor over the hall became possible. There was still a lingering feeling that a hall should be high, however, so they made this room some 9 ft.6ins (290 cms) high. The ceiling is quartered by beams with 7 inch wide hollow chamfers, with large step and run-out stops at the ends. The marks of the adze used for smoothing them can be easily seen. There was once a boss at the crossing of the beams in the middle of the room. All these details show that the ceiling was erected in the early or mid 16th century.

The Winsley Croft is yet another house which looks as if it consisted of a fifteenth or early sixteenth century hall with perhaps a crosswing at its south end, and its fire stack added later at the north end.

This ring, dating from c.1480, was found in a garden in nos. 126-128. The decoration, a crown above a heart on the front, and clasped hands on the back, suggests that it was originally given by Richard III to a supporter, perhaps of the Hungerford family.

4
The Later Tudor Years

O NE OF THE MANY interesting developments of the years following the dissolution of Shaftesbury Abbey in 1539 is the way in which some scraps of personal information about individual inhabitants begin to emerge and fill out the picture of the village, particularly when people of lesser status began to make wills. But it was still a time when we can seldom identify the homes even of people whose names are known. In some other villages, more prominent families such as the Longs at Semington were beginning to leave more detailed wills by the end of the fifteenth century. By contrast, the first known Winsley will, that of Thomas Ponting, dates only from 1542. About him we know only what his will tells us. One guesses that he had a small farm. Another very old will was Roger Deverell's in 1546; he probably lived in Frankley. These earliest known Winsley wills were rare and rather disappointing documents with little to say about the testator, his home or even its whereabouts. Gradually however we do meet examples that have more to tell. They all conform largely to a standard pattern of words which continued with little change for a century or more. Thomas Pontynge's will is unusual in some respects, but it illustrates what they were like. It has come down to us because a probate copy[1] was enrolled in the register of wills kept by the archdeacon of Salisbury. He was the man in charge of granting probate for a majority of the wills in the diocese. Someone, perhaps a scribe at Sarum, has added the date to Ponting's will, written out at great length. It takes several lines of script in Latin just to say 'The 18th of October 1542'. The will proper then follows in English in more or less the standard wording with some rather hilarious spelling. 'I Thomas Pontyng of the parysh of Wynsly beyng syke in boddy and hole in mynde make my testament and last wyll in forme and maner folowyng...'. Thomas bequeathes his sowle to God, 20 pence to Wynseley churchyard (for funeral expenses?), and makes other charitable donations to churches and to the poor, and then at last we come to his family bequests. He leaves his ploughing gear and a yoke of oxen to his eldest son Robert, ten sheepe and a Kowe to son

much as by your leave. One wonders if the trouble could have been that the stream from the Trows, running through Drewe's garden, was liable to run straight through his house instead. Whatever it was, he was ordered in no uncertain terms to return it to its old course before All Saints Day, October 30th; Fine 10s. The time permitted was short – the Court had only met on October 3rd.

Then there was the time when Drewse and four others, John Withye (perhaps at Manor Farm, Winsley), Richard Nutte, Richard Dicke and Richard Meade were 'presented by the homage' for getting their grain ground privately instead of using the customary manorial mill. They were fined 2s apiece.

By the beginning of the 18th century Drewe Druce's grandson Richard was certainly living at the Lyns at Turleigh, for we can compare the rooms named in Richard's inventory[15] with those in the present house. It shows that he occupied a substantial house with four rooms on the ground floor and three above, plus a 'little Chamber ' above that. There was also a long list of outbuildings[16]. From this it is easy to trace the house back, so we can be almost certain that Drewe Druse lived at the Lyns. Drewe was evidently quite a collector of farms. By 1614 or so, when the demesne land in Winsley belonging to the Bradford manor was being sold off,[17] he had collected five half-virgate farms, a large but not a vast estate. He died in 1621. Unfortunately his will is lost, as are the last few lines of the inventory; however the part we do have shows he had a six roomed house – the hall, the spence (a sort of larder, with pots and pans, cooking vessels, platters, candlesticks and of course the chamber pot), the parlour, with the chamber over it and the little chamber (only a coverlet, a bolster and a pair of blankets in this room) and the white house or dairy. And the rest is missing. This description could well fit the building as it would have been before the insertion of the first floor into the hall and the construction of the room above.

In more detail, we can fill in the story of the Lyns after Drew Druce's death. Shortly after, Drewe's son William made a good marriage. His bride was Elinor, daughter of Richard Dicke, a neighbour in Turleigh, who had helped with the making of Drew's inventory. The Dickes were clothiers, who probably came to Wiltshire from Reading, where they owned the Bear Inn. Richard had bought 'all that messuage, one halfe yardland, garden, orchard and Backeside' in Turlyn, probably at Turleigh Farm, the demesne farm along Green Lane. He also bought the fulling mill in Stoke and other property there[18] which he settled on his son Richard junior. At that time Richard senior probably lived at Turleigh Grange (as it now is), and rented the house opposite the Lyns, the one where James Barnes had lived. Richard left his two unmarried daughters £200 each, so perhaps Elinor, the eldest, had already been similarly endowed when she married. William Druce also spread his activities in another direction, becoming the earliest tanner in Turleigh of whom we have a record. The stream from the Trows, which we met before, running through the Lyns' garden, perhaps influenced the choice of the tannery site. Just below the garden the stream enters the mill pool, whence it could be released from time to time to drive the mill whenever enough water had accumulated. Tradition says this mill was used to grind the bark used in tanning.

The tomb of William and Elinor Druce, the oldest surviving one in Winsley churchyard, records the death of their first son Richard in 1630, aged five. A second son, also Richard, was to inherit the Lyns. William's will, made in 1659, shows him as more prosperous than his father. To his second surviving son he left the lease of Haugh Farm and two houses in Trowbridge and to his youngest son John the two other houses in Turleigh which had belonged to Drew Druce, plus £200. William also left to his daughter Anne a feather bed and £250. This was evidently to be a belated dowry for her marriage to Christopher Bailey, a clothier who held Wingfield manor and lived at Church Farm, the manor house of that village. In his will, William asks Christopher to make a suitable marriage settlement on his daughter. His youngest daughter received a legacy of only 1s, which must mean that she had already received her portion. William is also the most likely person to have added the parlour chimney and stack to the crosswing of the Lyns, containing a good mid 17th century fireplace on each floor.

The Lyns, we have seen, was inherited by William's son Richard Druce who, like his maternal grandfather was a clothier, and so the tannery business passed out of the family's ownership. His will does not involve the large sums of money that his father left, though he provided good marriage portions for three daughters and left silver spoons for each grandchild. Two daughters, Mary and Elinor were to share his brewing furnace. His third daughter Ann is not mentioned in the will, so perhaps she died before her father. The farm was a copyhold of Winsley Manor, and a copy of court roll survives granting it to Richard himself, with Mary and Elinor as the other two lives. Then, after Richard's death, the farm passed in turn to these two daughters Mary Tiley and Elinor Wilshire. In the copy of the Court roll dealing with this, the name of John Wiltshire junior, Elinor's son, was added as the third life on the deed. It is signed by Elizabeth Kent, lady of Winsley Manor[19]. After the death of this John Wilshire 'of Turley' the history of the farm is confused, and it reverted to the manor. Before 1820, however, it had passed to Ann Atwood, the great lady of Turley, who lived opposite the farm, at the house which now is Turleigh manor.

At Ashley too, there was one other large farm at the end of the 16th century. Little Ashley House was then at a different place from the present Little Ashley Farm. The old house, as the map below reveals, stood about a quarter of a mile west of the Ashley cross roads where the present farm stands. It was then in a large field on the south side of the road to Haugh, where, at least until recently, its remains could be seen in the form of a considerable scatter of ashlar stone blocks. It would have faced east, for the map shows an impressive avenue of trees in front of the house, running east, right across to Sterts Lane, the one which goes from the Ashley

Haigh

Nutt's, now Little Ashley

Winsley

Ashley in the early 18th century – where Little Ashley was and is.

crossroads, past Great Ashley and on to Winsley. Another old map shows the avenue continuing across that lane to join the lane that leads down past the Dog and Fox and on to Bradford.

The present Little Ashley Farm at the cross roads is clearly of considerable age too, with a semi-circular newel stair in a turret at the rear, and in the hall a ceiling whose high quality joists are all chamfered, with decorated stops of an early 17th century design. The house may well date from the previous century. It was the home of the Nutte family. Robert Nutte was one of the customary tenants listed in the Bradford rental of 1570, and the farm was long known as

Little Ashley Farm. It was called Nout's Tenement in the 1500s, and would have been renamed when the old Little Ashley House was pulled down.

Nutt's Tenement. He died in 1598, owning a lot of land that extended right out to Merfield at the north east corner of the Winsley tithing. He had a sheep flock of 31 wether ewes and hogges (one year olds) and several stalls of bees, which he kept in the bee-boles that are still to be seen in the angle between the front wall and the front porch of the house.

The old Great Ashley House has also disappeared completely, but the present farm is on the same site. Altogether, therefore, it has been possible to discover a great deal about the eastern end of the tithing, largely, of course because of the survival of early wills and their inventories.

Of Winsley village itself and its inhabitants at this period, in some ways less is known. A number of today's houses have been here since the sixteenth century, and are on much older farm sites. The Manor House, the Manor Farm, Burghope and Winsley Croft are all buildings looking as if they date back to the late fifteenth or sixteenth centuries. Nothing definite can be said about their history till a later period. It is a plausible guess that the two principal demesne farms of the Bradford manor, at Winsley Manor and Turley Farm, with their medieval origins, were both occupied by Richard Meade in 1600 at the turn of the century. Again, the Manor Farm may then have belonged to the Hendy family. The old 'Winsley House', as it was called in later centuries, may have been another early house, but may equally have been built at a later date. It occupied a site close to Dorothy House, which replaced the old house when that was demolished in 1902; all we have is a 19th century photograph showing a house perhaps of around 1600.

Turning to smaller houses, a church terrier of 1608 states that there then was a cottage for the curate on the north side of the church. It would then have been occupied by Henry Redman, senior but seems to have been taken down around 1700 when we had an absentee curate, James Butter. Succeeding Redman in about 1688, he became rector of Ditteridge near Box in 1694, while still remaining Winsley's curate. His name is commemorated at Butters Cottage[20] next to Haugh Farm. This he bought in 1688, though he himself seems to have moved later to Ditteridge.

Smaller cottages, timber framed and thatched, must have been fairly numerous. Some were probably scattered out in the fields or on the waste, but it is clear that many others were clustered together in the village. This was highlighted by a disaster that struck John Wilshere in 1596. One winter night, he had the misfortune to overturn his boiling furnace when he was doing some brewing, and the court record says this was 'to the great danger of burning down his house and those of other householders'. These houses must all have been close together. It is not clear if the house actually caught fire, but he was ordered to repair it – that sounds a bit of an unnecessary order! – and not to do it again on pain of a fine of 40s, roughly the cost of building a cottage in those days.

In the four years covered by the Bradford manor roll in the 1590s, a number of new cottages were erected, each with a curtillage – a yard or garden – adjoining the house. At least two of them were built on the village waste; William Walter's new cottage had a curtillage 63 feet long and 40 feet wide, whereas Maria Wilkyns' was much smaller, only 32 ft. by 12. Then there was Thomasina Atkyns who in 1598 was granted for her widowhood a new, recently built cottage[21] at Conkwell. That is the earliest known mention we have of any building there. Her garden was larger, 80 feet by 30 and her rent was 12d. Later in the same year the lord of the manor granted another recently built cottage to Henry Marshman, with its garden and two acres of land in The Sands on the north side of Winsley Church. On top of the rent he had to perform the customary feudal works and services.[22]

Henry Marshman and Roger Walter, William's brother, were also named with several others in another Court Order that year[23]. 'It was ordered (in Latin of course) at this Court that they, being tenants of the manor, did not 'labant' (this Latin is probably an abbreviation of 'lavabant' i.e. in English 'they shall wash'), – Anglice (in English) 'wett their chaynes' – in lez troughes next to a certein spring in Winnesley and that they shall 'mundant', Anglice 'make clean', the same les troughes under a penalty of 2s for each of them for each offence.' Evidently a weaver's warp was called Chains until not so long ago in Somerset. Presumably the Trows were the same row of basins we know, filled by that same stream by the roadside at Turleigh.

The Manor was obviously concerned that the houses and barns be kept in good repair. There are frequent orders to the tenants to carry out 'sufficient repairs and maintenance' to the timber and thatch of their houses with the usual penalties if the work was not completed by the next meeting of the Court. For larger repairs it was normal for the householder to ask the court to allot him two trees, to be supplied by the bailiff. The system was sometimes abused, of course, as when one Edward White used his allotted trees for some other purpose – probably he sold them. Another frequent offence liable to lead to a heavy fine was sub letting a house. 'It is ordered at this Court that James Wilshere remove John Whippe his subtenant out of his house before the next feast of St John

The Trows at Turleigh.

the Baptist on pain of a fine of 20s.' Were they afraid that Whippe would become a pauper, a burden on the parish?[24] Anyway, a couple of years later Robert Huntley was being ordered in the same way to remove his subtenant – none other than John Whippe! Quite likely Whippe was a good farm worker to have in your household (even if the fine for being caught had now gone up to 40s.).

With so much building work going on in the village, William Venell, the carpenter must have been a busy man. He lived at a cottage in the back lane, now no. 141. Quite likely it was timber framed in those days, but later refaced in stone. The nineteenth century photograph gives a good view of it – the small square one, gabled to the front and back of the main ridge is of a typical 16th century plan. Its neighbour on the left is joined to it, and is probably of much the same date. But, rather surprisingly, the two houses are separated, upstairs at least, [25] each with its own timber framed wall, about a foot apart. Clearly, it seems that the two cottages were originally timber framed with a gap between them and only became parts of one building when they were later refaced in stone. Another long low cottage (no.142) abuts on the back of Vennell's house, blocking his old rear window. It must have been built rather later. Vennell's house has a large fireplace on the right of the one downstairs room. There now is a through passage between it and its left hand neighbour. In the loft the rafters of the original roof remained till recently, with those of a more modern higher roof above them.

Vennell the carpenter made his will in 1617, and his inventory reveals that by the standards of the day, the house was well equipped. Only one rather small room is mentioned[26] – perhaps there was a similar one over it reached by a ladder – it is a mystery how there could be space for the various bulky things in the room, not to mention William and his wife Joan, their four sons and five daughters all living there. Fortunately the three pigs, cock, hen and 8 chicks lived outside, in the yard. The valuable items were William's working tools, the three bedsteads, cauldrons and crocks. Several later generations of the family were still carpenters, but later they changed to weaving. The

In the lane, formerly Vennals, then (above) and now (opposite page, top) . It goes back at least to the 1500s.

cottage is drawn on the 1727 manorial map, named Venals. The head of the family at that time was another John Vennel, who married Mary Dagger. Their only son, another John, had six spinster sisters to maintain, so he never married. However Ann, the youngest sister, married a family apprentice Walter Simkins, who in due course inherited the property. Walter is said to have built a couple of the neighbouring cottages as well [27] in the early 1800s.

Finally, and nothing to do with Winsley, the court minutes for the 31st March 1599 for the Borough of Bradford have the following entry:

> And that the inhabitants of the said borough shall sufficiently repair and replace in its customary location le Cuckingstole within the foresaid borough before the third day of May next ensuing, on pain of a fine of 20s. to the lord of the manor.

That should have improved their morals [28].

5
The Manor

WHEN WE SPEAK of the manor in a village or town, we instinctively think of a fairly large house, the manor house. In early days it would be a major farmhouse, the home of a country gentleman. But related to this is a secondary meaning; the manor as a single unit for the local administration of the whole or part of an estate. It might or might not contain the residence of the holder. He, the lord of the manor, held it directly of the king, who granted him certain well defined rights and powers.[1] In this sense, throughout the Middle Ages the only true manor in and around Bradford was the very large estate granted by King Ethelred to Shaftesbury Abbey. From time to time lesser estates within that manor achieved some degree of independence, sometimes calling themselves manors or one might say sub-manors. Even as far back as the twelfth century the Shaftesbury surveys suggest that Atworth, the tithing furthest away from the manor farm, that is, Barton Farm, was being run in some ways as a separate unit within the manor. Later on for instance, Atworth had quite a large tithe barn of its own. Again, we have seen that by the mid fourteenth century the glebe land belonging to Bradford church had been made into a separate Prebendal or Rectory manor. How far this was independent of the main manor is not altogether clear – it does not seem to have been clear even to the people of those days! At this time, too, South Wraxall,[2] held by the Poyntz family, was independent enough to have had its own separate account rolls; unfortunately these are now lost, but they certainly survived until quite recently. It would have been interesting to see how they differ from those of the main manor, to which they paid an annual rent of fifteen shillings. And in the fifteenth century two other Bradford families had estates independent enough to become known as Hall's Manor and Rogers' Manor, though of course they were still definitely under the overall control of the Bradford manor. Much the same goes for a manor of Ashley and Budbury, in those days within the Winsley tithing.

By this time, too, the idea of a manor had changed, the new definition being that a property was a manor if and only if its owner held a regular court baron which his tenants had to attend. Technically a court baron had jurisdiction in its property matters.[3] One cannot always tell whether these sub-manors came under this heading or not. The Bradford manor and the Hundred certainly still held all their traditional courts.

Winsley, (apart from Ashley, Budbury and the prebendal manor holdings) remained an integral part of Bradford manor at least until the early seventeenth century. Throughout all that time Bradford Manor must have had two large demesne farms here, at Winsley and at Turleigh, the Winsley one being the chief farm in the village, centred on the Conigre field which has become our cricket ground. The site of the demesne farmhouse must have been close to the present Manor House, if not actually at the same place. The earliest hint of there being a Winsley manor comes several years after 1600; it is noticeable that even in the 18th century the main farm of the manor was still usually known as the Upper Farm, the Lower Farm being the Turleigh one. The core of the present manor house, with its walls of thickness 30 – 32 inches, was probably built in the sixteenth century, maybe with a rebuild of about 1550. The south eastern wing, with 36' walls could be earlier.

We have not been able to find out who were the farm's earlier occupants, but a likely candidate about the mid century was John Wilshere 'of the Down',[4] who died in 1574. His will shows that he was a prosperous farmer. At that time there were several other men in the village also called John Wilshere, so nicknames were needed to distinguish them. The Down is an area belonging to the Winsley demesne farm, on the brow of the hill, between the Conigre and Turleigh.

After the dissolution of Shaftesbury Abbey in 1539, its estates passed into the king's hands and over the succeeding years the Bradford manor (including the outlying villages) was granted to a succession of owners, firstly in 1546 to Sir Edward Bellingham[5], and after his death, to members of the Herbert family of Wilton House, the Earls of Pembroke. Then in 1576 Queen Elizabeth granted the reversion of the whole Bradford manor to her Secretary of State Sir Francis Walsingham. In other words this grant was not to come into effect until after the expiry of the previous lease to the Herberts. Walsingham died in 1590, and 'according to the customs of the manor', his widow Ursula then held the estate for her life. Sir Francis had settled the manor on their daughter Frances in 1584 on her marriage to Sir Philip Sidney. She therefore would automatically take over the Bradford manor on her mother's death. Sidney was killed at the battle of Zutphen two years after their marriage, leaving his widow heavily in debt. A few years later Frances remarried, her second husband being the Queen's favourite, the Earl of Essex. It was to prove an unfortunate choice as

Essex was executed for treason in 1601, leaving his widow still further in debt. By 1607 Frances had married her third husband, the Irish peer Ricard Bourke, Earl of Clanricard[6], for we read that in that year the Earl held a Court Baron of the manor of Bradford with one John Kent as his Steward.

By then, Frances had acquired a second link with Bradford, a lease of the Prebendal manor coming to her in a rather devious way. Henry VIII had of course seized this church manor at the dissolution of the Abbey, and shortly afterwards he granted it to the Dean and Chapter of the new diocese of Bristol which was then being set up.[7] And in 1545 the Dean and Chapter gave the management of the estate to William Webbe of Bradford and his wife as bailiffs, leasing it to them for life. However, about forty years later the Dean was persuaded, no doubt under some royal pressure, to assign the remainder of the lease of this Bradford rectory to Queen Elizabeth[8] as she wished to grant it too to Walsingham. And in the following year Walsingham in turn made this lease over to his daughter Frances. Here we again meet John Kent, for as well as being the Steward of the manor of Bradford, he had for several years been Steward of the Dean of Bristol's Prebendal manor of Bradford.

John Kent (1558 – 1630)[9] was a man of many parts. Born in Cheshire, he clearly had a legal training and, moving to Wiltshire about 1580, he became a prominent citizen of Devizes. He held numerous offices there over the years, among them being town clerk from 1592 till 1626. Here he left records most meticulously kept and written in his own neat but very minute hand. He was Mayor of Devizes in 1602 – 3 and represented the borough in parliament from 1597-1601, again in 1620-21 and in 1624. Kent is also remembered for a remarkable bound volume of all the Charters of the Borough[10] from the first one granted by the Empress Matilda in 1141 down to his own time. Many of them are illustrated with portraits of the kings and queens, which some think were Kent's own work. His gifts of organisation and neatness are best shown in his work as Clerk of the Peace for Wiltshire from 1601 to 1626.[11] It is to him that we owe the survival of a fine series of Quarter Sessions records, with minutes minutely kept, and the writs signed for the first time by the clerk. Kent's tiny handwriting enabled him to get four lines of text on to a parchment strip only ¾ of an inch wide. Besides being, as we have seen, steward of the Bradford manor and of the Prebendal manor, John Kent was also steward of a number of other important estates, in particular those of the Earl of Hertford[12].

He married Mary, the daughter of Thomas Wiatt of Calne in 1585, when he was 27. It was a happy marriage, for when he made his will in 1629 and looked back over their forty four years together, he wrote of 'Mary, who hath ever been unto me a most faithful and comfortable yoke-fellow'. The Kents seem always to have lived in Devizes, at no.16 in the Market Place. This they rebuilt, putting their initials I M K (John and Mary Kent) with the date 1610 on the front gable.

Their eldest son John [II] was born in 1587, and a daughter Mary and sons Thomas and Samuel followed. In 1611, John [II] married Ann, daughter of Jerome Poticary, a clothier of Stockton in the Wylye valley. In the following January Ann gave birth to a son, John [III], who was baptised in Devizes. In March, the young couple visited Stockton, but while they were there John [II] fell ill and died of a 'burning fever'. He was only 25. So little John[III] was left fatherless at the age of six weeks. For the moment John Kent's second son Thomas became his father's principal heir, though it is clear that from the beginning John took great interest in his grandson's upbringing. It was presumably at this

Portrait of Frances, Lady Walsingham.

time that the date stone shown in the picture was erected on the Winsley farmhouse – it is said however to have been moved fairly recently to its present position over a door in the kitchen. There are two inscriptions on it, I M K 1612, standing for John and Mary Kent, 1612, and T ☐ K, Thomas and Katherine – Thomas Kent had married Katherine Reade, daughter of the vicar of Bradford. We do not know whether Thomas and Katherine lived at Winsley manor house; it is probable that they did, for of their children only the eldest, Peter, was baptised in Devizes. The others could have been baptised at Winsley, though we cannot confirm this, as the village baptismal records (Bishop's Transcripts) do not survive before 1623. The date stone confirms that old John Kent had acquired a number of Winsley properties by that year, although the stone itself may not have been erected till later.

Because of his position as Steward to the Clanricards, John Kent would have been aware of the financial difficulties besetting them, and of their plan to alleviate them by selling off much of the Bradford manor. Taking advantage of this, Kent was able to provide for his grandson's future by purchasing that manor's property in Winsley.

The amount of land John Kent was proposing to buy was less than we would probably expect. For one thing, a century or more before this, the whole eastern part of the Winsley tithing had been divided off to become the manor of Ashley and Budbury; and it was even earlier than that the parsonage land, much of it in Winsley, had become the Parsonage or Rectory manor. Other holdings, too, were then being disposed of by the Clanricards; for instance in 1610,[13] they sold a large farm at Turleigh to Richard Dicke. What remained for the sale to Kent amounted to 16½ yardlands, perhaps some 400 to 600 acres[14], only a small fraction of Winsley's 3,000 acres. The sale deeds show that, perhaps for financial reasons, Kent bought the property in two instalments a couple of years apart[15]. In those days holdings were still made up of numerous scattered strips of land, in the old medieval way, so it is almost impossible to locate any of the farms except the largest. As a guess, the two demesne farms of Bradford manor at Winsley and Turleigh must surely have been the ones described in the sale documents, the one as 'one messuage and one yardland and certain Overlands in Winsley, sometymes in the occupation of Richard Meade' and the other as 'one messuage and one yardland at Turley', also previously held by Meade.[16] Meade died in 1612, and before the main sale, John Kent had already taken over the leases of these farms. The sale was also to include the farms of several men we have previously met – Richard Guydinge (a cottage called Lockscote) and Drewe Druce (five half-yardlands in Turlinge, Haughe and Winnesley). And in the second instalment of the sale was one of the biggest of them all – 'a messuage, half a hide and one yardland, containing 100 acres of land, meadow, pasture and wood in Winnesley and Turley', occupied by John Wythie. That ought to be identifiable – could it be the present Manor Farm?

All this property, being held directly – 'in chief' – by the Clanricards from the king, could not be sold without obtaining a licence from the Crown. There may have been a further little difficulty to overcome in this sale, because Kent had interests with both the parties involved. He was not only the purchaser, but at the same time the steward to the vendors.

The sale is described in a set of ten parchment indentures now at the county record office. (The bundle includes several duplicates and 18th century copies as well). Each party to the sale was associated with a legal team, the Clanricards' headed by Sir Henry Yelverton, the king's Solicitor General and John Kent's by Nicholas Hide, a future Lord Chancellor. The others in this group, who were to become Kent's trustees for the property, were Devizes clothiers, (with legal qualifications, one presumes), two of them connected to Kent by marriage.[17] The sale of the first half of the property involved three deeds, the first in 1614, a lease for 99 years from the Earl and Countess with their lawyers to Kent's trustees, effectively putting the property at the king's disposal. Then came the royal 'Licence to Alienate', authorising the transfer of ownership to Ken and his team. And thirdly a 'Word of Feoffment' in which the Clanricards assign their property rights to John Kent. All this was then enrolled in Chancery by a 'Final Concord'. Two years later the whole rigmarole had to be repeated for the second half of the sale. To crown it all, in the last indenture John Kent and his trustees set out how the estate was to be managed.

the Chase and it sounds as if it used to be a larger area. And the High Way was the old name for the path past the Chase, past the cricket ground and on down to Turleigh and Avoncliff, with the Down Close on the east side. The Hulks is a forgotten name; alternatively called the Hillocks, it became Hollybush Tyning and would now be somewhere in the Tyning Estate. And Thomas Chapman of Bradford, though his land was not being exchanged at this time, did get involved a year later. He was a Handlesetter, a trade belonging to a process in the finishing of fine cloth, whose nap was raised for shearing by drawing wooden frames across its face. These frames, called handles, had teasel heads set in them.[29]

It was at this time, in 1727, that John Thresher had his map of the manor drawn probably to show how the new fields were replacing the old strip countryside, though we cannot be sure how far the map was recording the earlier situation rather than the 1727 one. As well as showing all Thresher's manor lands, the map shows a considerable area bearing the name Moses Cottle. He was clearly a prosperous farmer. Formerly living somewhere at Haugh, he had recently moved to Winsley House, where Dorothy House now is. There were important land exchanges between Thresher and Cottle, leading to several new farms on the map. It was by no means straightforward arrangement, and I hope to be excused for not attempting to sort them out here. The scheme will be found in the notes at the end of this chapter [30].

When Edward Thresher died in 1725, his son John gave up a successful career at the Bar to take over the management of his father's business. John, too, had married into the Long family; his wife was Ellin, daughter of Henry Long of Melksham.[31] Four daughters were born of the marriage, and the family held Winsley manor for the next century. The eldest daughter, Ellen Thresher made a good marriage. In 1755 she became the second wife of Sir Bourchier Wrey of Tawstock in Devon, who is remembered as a member of the Dilettanti Club. Her marriage settlement included a complete survey of the Thresher property, which she was to share equally with her three sisters.[32] The marriage of the third sister Elizabeth gives us a rare glimpse of some family affairs. Her husband Robert Colebrook, of a well to do family, was evidently a poor character, for already in 1765 he was described as 'late of Chilham Castle, Kent, and late His Majesty's Consul at the Canton of Bern'. Elizabeth's younger sister Mary let the cat out of the bag when, in a draft of a will a few years later, she expressed her feelings strongly – 'my meaning is to make them entirely independent, particularly my sister Colebrook, from any possibility of her husband claiming or having any right to what part falls to her share. Mr. B (the solicitor) will be so good to express my sentiments thro'out properly and secure for my sister Colebrook not to have any trouble from Mr.C.' As things worked out, she

The Seven Stars.

outlived him, and we read of her second and happier marriage to John Crossdill, a leading cellist in the king's orchestra.[33]

At this time the Manor House was again being leased out as the farmhouse of the Winsley Farm, the tenants being Richard and Charles Broad, father and son. The Broad family had come to Winsley in about 1690 from Box, where they had been stonemasons and carpenters. The first stage of the building of Dyrham Park House was growing at this time, and it was at Box that Richard Broad quarried much of the fine stone he used for his work on the architraves of the doors and windows, and on the balustraded parapet at the top of the east face of that building.[34] Richard's elder brother Cornelius became landlord of the Seven Stars at Winsley, which also belonged to the manor. Richard and Charles were at the Manor until 1771, when Richard was 77. Before the new tenant John Heal came in, 'extraordinary repairs' were needed. Tiling, plastering and carpentry had to be done, and the field walls mended – a sad tale of neglect. William Taylor, the blacksmith, whose forge stood next to No.155 Church Cottages, charged £4 13s 8d for his 'Ironwork at Farm House and Gates to ye Farm', and Aaron Pickwick was paid £4 11s for thatching, followed by 17s.7d a couple of years later for rethatching the Seven Stars[35] after a severe storm.

Long before this, though, John Thresher and his wife had died, and it is interesting to compare their wills[36]. John's bequests were very even handed, for he left £12,000 to be equally divided between his daughters, after making provision for his wife. The manor estate was to be administered by trustees, some of their Long uncles, again equally for the girls. John's wife Ellen, who died of smallpox in the 1753 epidemic, had different ideas. The eldest girl, also Ellen, was to get £1000 and the best jewellery – 'all my roses or stars of brilliant Diamonds for the stays, my diamond Solitaire, my brilliant Diamond Girdle buckle, my mother of pearl snuff box set in gold and 2 of my diamond rings'. Then Dionysia and Elizabeth were to have rather less, '£200, my diamond earrings consisting of a toppanot and 3 drops to each, on condition that she deliver to her sister Elizabeth the earrringe she has at present and a gold watch' – and so on. And young Mary, who was then about three years old, had to be content with one gold snuffbox and a few rings. However, she outlived all her sisters, eventually acquiring all the manor, and living in a house in the Circus in Bath. She died in about 1816, leaving all her property to her nieces, Ellen Wrey's children.[37]

By 1825 it was decided to sell the Winsley estate; copies of the sale particulars survive, written in an estate agent's usual glowing terms. The manor was said to have been a 643 acre property, worth £1,000 a year. A letter written soon after the sale shows that the proceeds were over £30,000.[38]

The Manor House and a certain amount of land were bought by John Hayes Dunkin and James Baber. Baber was the manager at Murhill quarry; stone must always have been quarried in Winsley, but during the building of the Kennet and Avon Canal at the beginning of the 19th century the quarries were enlarged and the tramway built from the quarry down to a new wharf on the canal. After the completion of the canal, stone could be sent by water to London and elsewhere. Baber lived at Murhill House, which he probably built, and the manor continued to be leased. According to the 1851 census, the tenant of the manor by then was the Rev. R. L. Cogan, vicar of the then newly created parish of Winsley, who moved the following year to Lambourne House. In 1872 the tenant was the Rev. Charles Parfitt [39] who was probably responsible for the use of an upstairs room at the Manor as a chapel, as tradition asserts. By 1899 the Manor House had been bought by W.E. Knatchbull, who added the large extension to the west end. After his death, the Manor house was divided between his daughters, who were living there until 1985.

The Manor house, as it stands now, consists of a principal range, say four bays long, with four main rooms on each floor. This was probably built in the early 17th or late 16 th century, for it has the two light, round-headed windows of the period. Some of these, mainly in the living rooms in the western half, were later replaced by large Victorian sash windows. The house faces roughly south with a stair turret at the back, and next to that a more recent kitchen. It has now been divided into two separate dwellings, and in the last century a high block was added at the west end. On the south face of the house's east room a short wing projects, running somewhat east of south. It is about one room long and not quite as high as the main house. Its walls are rather thicker than those of the main house (36' against 32'), so it may have been part of an older building. And to the east of the main range and aligned with it, a short distance away, there is a large 19th century detached barn, now converted to a dwelling, with a group of farm buildings adjoining. Inside the house, the 1612 datestone with the Kents' initials is now the lintel of a door leading from the kitchen to the old main range.

Several notable interior features come from an early seventeenth century four poster bed. Its tester now forms the ceiling of the porch and its head has been made into the overmantel around the fireplace and other features in the dining room. Was this perhaps John Kent's own bed? Alternatively, the traditional village story is that the bed was a gift from King Charles II to Jane Lane, who escorted him as far as Bristol during his escape from the country after his defeat at the battle of Worcester and his adventure, hidden in the Boscobel Oak. If so, how did the bed come to be in Winsley, for Jane Lane does not seem to have had any link with our village? One may perhaps construct a far-fetched story to explain it as follows: – by the end of the king's reign the Lanes thought they could safely dispose of the bed – 'What'll us do with that

The Manor House: a. Front view

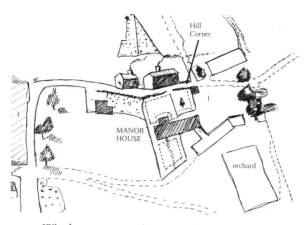

Winsley manor, as it was on the 1727 map.

there old thing?'. Suppose it then came into the hands of Sir John Knight, the mayor of Bristol, whose daughter Elizabeth married John Kent IV. Here then is a link with Winsley Manor. But this story contains too many weak links.

Looking now at the 1727 map, drawn for John Thresher, the picture is rather different and sets problems of interpretation. The plans of the manorial and the parsonage buildings at that time are shown in outline. The main house, less the kitchen and other recent additions, has not changed since. The chief difference is that a large building – shall we call it a barn – about the same size as the main house, but aligned north east to south west, stood across the outer end of the old south east wing. More accurately, its orientation was at right angles to that wing. And, though it is not quite clear, the map seems to show the house's south east wing as belonging not to the house but to this 'barn', which must have been a prominent building in 1727. Of course it has completely disappeared now. A number of possible explanations of this barn come to mind. A first idea is that it might be the 'new barn' mentioned in John Kent's 1627 lease of the manor to Willyam Allen. Or was it a forerunner of the farmhouse itself? Wasn't it a bit too large for that? And if it was too large, was it much older? Dare one mention the word 'tithe barn'! We may compare with the situation at Atworth, where a medieval tithe barn still stands for collecting the tithe crops locally before taking them down to the great central barn at Bradford. Was there a similar situation in the other tithings – Wraxall and the rest?

6
The Seventeenth Century Growth

THERE WERE CONSIDERABLE CHANGES during the 17th century on the hillside above the town in the no-mans-land between Bradford and Winsley, whose top belonged to Budbury farm in our tithing. In sorting this out, a continuing source of confusion is that of course the whole of Winsley tithing then lay within the parish of Bradford.

When John Leland, King Henry VIIIth's 'Antiquary', visited the town of Bradford in about 1533 on one of his journeys round England,[1] he arrived by the Corsham road and came into the town by way of the Hermitage, as St Mary Tory was then called. A deed in 1588 calls it St Leonard's Hermitage in Budbury.[2] The tithing boundary must have run across the hillside somewhere below. Leland could look down on the houses of Church Street, and the church itself with Thomas Horton's new Church House to the east of it. In between was Horton's own new house with a manorial dove cote on the hillside just above. To the left, half way up the hill, was the mansion house of Rogers' Manor, later to become Methuen's and known as the Priory since Victorian times. One wonders how far the town's houses had crept up Market Street in Leland's time. Apart from that, the whole of the slope was perhaps a patchwork of orchards, gardens and pasture, not yet firmly assigned either to the town or to the tithing. We cannot be sure what path Leland would have taken on his way down into the town but the most likely way seems to have been down the Wellpath. That is surely a very old path, for at the end of the 17th or early in the 18th century the new houses at the top of Tory were built right across it.

At least until the eighteenth century the chief road from Bradford towards Winsley seems to have followed the line of present Newtown road across the hillside as far as the foot of Wine Street. In those days the land between Wine Street and the Wellpath, till recently the brewery site, used to be known as Catshill, or earlier as Cats Hole Hill.[3] It belonged to the Budbury manor which, with the Hermitage, had been acquired in 1578 by John Blanchard. From the last years of that century, Blanchard had started granting new leases for a number of his cottages and for the erection of new ones here at Catshill.[4] Among the papers dealing with these is an unusual group to do with a lease to one Rychard Marchant. Without knowing the background story it is not very clear what was going on. They start in 1607 with a petition to the Justices of the Peace, sitting at the Quarte Sessions in Salisbury. A group of Bradford parishioners, including the three Church-wardens and a number of prominent clothiers – John Yewe and Walter Yerbury among others – were making a plea on behalf of Marchant, whom they call a man of honest life and conversation who had no habitation of his own and was impoverished by the Great Rent he had to pay. They say he had the goodwill of the lord of the manor of Sudburie (surely Budburie) and had, according to the Law, obtained the lease (does this mean 'obtained permission'?) to build and erect a cottage on the 'wast grownd' of that manor. The petitioners beseech their Worships to 'grant to our poor neighbour Warrant for the erection thereof'. It states the Court had given Marchant Licence to erect one cottage, and evidently ask that this should be 'withoutt incurring the forfeiture mentioned in the Statute against the erecting and mayntaining cottages'. This may refer to an Act of 1589 laying down that all new cottages should have at least four acres of land attached, but this could be relaxed for cottages for the very poor.[5] So now Blanchard leases the cottage lately built by Marchant, where he now dwells, with a little garden and a backsyde (backyard) adjoining it. The sad end of the story is that Marchant probably never completed his cottage, for, a year or two later he died, and in a fresh lease to his widow Cycely and their daughter Margaret, the cottage is still 'now erecting and late building'.

After Blanchard's death, a deed in 1627 shows there was then an active quarry at Catshill.[6] A further feature adding to the attraction of this Catshill site was no doubt the nearby Ladywell spring [7], so valuable a source of pure water for the town's later development. These new cottages, still separated from the town by open country, were naturally called Newtown. In the early 17th century there was some further building to the west of Wine Street in the angle between that and the Turleigh road and some also in the Wellclose area below Newtown, across from the Seven Stars inn. Even in 1842, when the Bradford boundary had moved further north beyond Budbury Farm on the hilltop, the TA map still shows these parts of the hillside bore TA numbers in the Winsley schedule, assigning them to that tithing rather than to the town.

From 1657, after the Rogers family had moved away from Bradford, their town mansion came into the ownership of the Methuens. With the latter's clothing business beginning to flourish there, they leased out numerous plots of land in Tory, Middle Rank and Newtown for their workforce to build themselves cottages.[8] The numbering of this new Methuen estate in the TA shows these too were once a detached part of Winsley.

The main road, having reached Catshill, went on, surprisingly in view of the steep gradient, up Wine Street, only turning west towards Winsley on reaching the top. Even when the road through Winsley was turnpiked in 1751, apparently it still took this Wine Street route, for a toll bar was mentioned there in the Turnpike Trust minutes of 1817.[9] Other roads leading off this one were smaller, just bridle ways or lanes. The former Budbury Lane used to lead eastwards from the top of Wine Street more or less along the line of the present Winsley Road, but then turning across to Budbury Farm. So in the early times it would have been in the Winsley tithing as far as Budbury Manor, though its route further eastwards, if indeed it did go on, is more doubtful. In the Tithe Map the Winsley/Bradford boundary ran along the western part of this lane before turning north up Huntingdon Street. The road is not mentioned as turnpiked in the Act of 1798 but in the 1819 Act[10] we find it among the roads named as belonging to the Trust – and, as I interpret it, it was deemed a road due for turnpiking. The Act reads 'The Lane called Budbury Lane leading from the said old road at the top of Palmers Lane (the old name for the upper part of Wine Street) to join the new road at Says Green'.[11] Christ Church evidently stands on part of Say's Green.

The lower road past Belcombe to Turleigh was just another lane until the 1820s. Leaving the houses at Catshill, it crosses what seems likely to have been an area of common grazing, later to be part of the Hare Knap open field. It then took a fairly direct route towards Turleigh, remaining rather higher up the hillside than it does nowadays, up the middle of the field to the right of the present road after passing Belcombe (occasionally written Velcombe in the 1500s). Consequently, when John Yerbury built his new house at Belcombe Brook (now Belcombe Court) the green field site he chose practically straddled the old road, which must have cut right across his new garden. So Yerbury blocked the old road, constructing a ha-ha to mark out the west end of his garden. Thorpe's 1743 map shows how this section of the road had been diverted, in the first instance just moving the section blocked by Yerbury's garden southwards to follow round outside his garden wall. At some time in

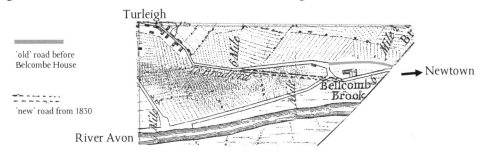

Turleigh

'old' road before
Belcombe House

'new' road from 1830

Newtown

Belcombe
Brook

River Avon

How the Turley lane from Bradford may have developed.

the early 1800s the road was probably turnpiked, and the section of the road west of Yerbury's garden was realigned along its present straight course, removing the two awkward bends and improving the view from the house. At the west end of this new section there still is the junction with the old road, and a bit further on we find a stretch of narrower, winding road. Can that be a short surviving stretch of the old one? And where the road reaches Turleigh, Ivor Slocombe[12] has found evidence for a toll bar across the road.

What may be a distant echo of the old road lives on in a 'tall dog story'[13] told a few years ago by an old Winsley stonemason and storyteller, of how someone, returning with his dog from Bradford on a winter evening, paused for a while, looking over the gate to the ha-ha of the Belcombe garden. He told a tale of seeing a woman wearing a cloak of a style long past, coming down the middle of the field as if from Turleigh. Did he know that she was following the probable line of the old road? When she came to the ha-ha, instead of turning down it, she crossed straight over it as if on the old ground level, and carried on towards the house. Looking down, he saw his dog's hair was standing on end and it ran away as fast as it could go. Recovering, the man made his way on home, to find the dog shivering on the doorstep.

The Tidcombe Family and the Haugh Farms

A FAMILY who became prominent at Winsley in this turbulent century were the descendents of Michael Tidcombe or Titcombe who, like John Kent, was a Devizes lawyer. Members of the family are to be found in various parts of the county over the years that follow. Michael's eldest son Edward lived at Estcott near Urchfont for many years, but we find his grandson at Atworth, where at the end of the century there lived another Edward Tidcombe, who was a surgeon.

The Tidcombe's connection with Winsley began when Michael senior's younger son, another Michael (1592 – 1662) acquired Great Ashley by marrying Susanna, a daughter of its owner John Blanchard. This was in 1626, by which time both John Blanchard and his son John junior, her brother, were dead, and had left their estates to Susanna and her surviving sisters. So in due course Michael inherited this estate as well as Little Ashley 'in the right of his wife'. The two Ashleys, it will be remembered, had long been occupied by John and Anthony Druce as Blanchard's tenants. John Druce, still living at Great Ashley, now became Tidcombe's tenant.

Nine years after her marriage Susanna Tidcombe died, leaving as heir her son Edward, then aged 7 years 8 months and 5 days. Of her possessions, not one but two I.P.M's[14] were taken each giving quite a full description of her land at Great Ashley. On the whole they agree with each other, though there are a number of surprising differences between the two of them. In the second I.P.M., for instance, 'Great Ashley Howse' has been transformed into 'Grate Ughley Howe'! Should we perhaps blame this one on the imagination of the editor of the modern edition of the documents? The fields are all listed, but of course most of the names have changed over the years since then. It is not easy to locate them, apart from a group close to the farm, such as Barne Close, Well Close and Broad Meade, 15 acres in all. But what about 'Oxen Sitting'? The origin of the name, whatever it meant, was probably forgotten and lost long ago; the field was, I guess, somewhere next to Longcrofte, but that too, alas, is now unknown. Though many of the fields were around the farm, it is clear that others were further away, some even in Kingsfield and in Woollies' Field, north east of Bradford. Susanna had eight cottages too, which went with the farm. Their occupants are named but they are of course strangers to us[15].

The other half of John Blanchard's estate went to Susanna's younger sister Joyce Allen, who died two years after Susanna. She was the wife of Thomas Allen, a 'wolin draper' in Devizes. Her I.P.M.[16] shows the estate had been divided very fairly between the sisters, so evenly, in fact that the fields in the two shares were confusingly intermingled. It does not seem possible to find where the Allens were living locally. Her home was a messuage or cottage called Gregorie's Howse.

Michael Tidcombe acquired Haugh Farm about the same time. During these early centuries a number of farms, among them Haugh Potticks, Upper Haugh and Parsonage farms were all simply referred to as 'Haugh Farm'. There is however enough other evidence to show that Tidcombe's farm was indeed the one that we still know as Haugh Farm. The tenant, John Druce, son of William Druce the Turleigh tanner, lived there in a two up – two down house (or perhaps it was a larger house he was sharing with his brother). It was a large farm, with 71 acres of it arable land which he held under a lease from Robert Shaa of Hinton Charterhouse. Shaa later sold it to Michael Tidcombe; Michael himself, however, still continued to live in Devizes.

The 1630s and 40s were years of much unrest, brewing up towards the coming civil war. Even so, one imagines that most of the troubles of the time would have bypassed a village like Winsley. Rather than by the big national issues, it would be more affected by the happenings such as having to contribute to the upkeep of the Parliamentary garrison that was at Great Chalfield. In 1645-6 the Winsley contribution, 'brought in to the garrison from there', was 674 lb of cheese, 52 bushels of oats and 36½ bushels of wheat. And 5 labourers worked for 29 days·[17]. Writing of Freshford in these years, Alan Dodge[18] stresses the influence the growing clothing mills had on the prosperity of that village. One assumes that similarly in Winsley the age-old Avoncliff Mill prospered, though the evidence for growth at that period is lacking. The village life would remain dominated by the agriculture, with spinning and weaving as largely cottage activities dominated by the Bradford clothiers. Shortly after 1700 there was a sale of the two mills, one 'at Ancliff alias Ankley in the parish of Westwood', and the other, on the Winsley side, 'lyeing att Avonclift, in the parish of Bradford'[19] At that time there was an acre of land called the Rackhams next to the mill house – the racks for drying the cloth would have been there. And there were two mills adjoining, under one roof, a water grist mill and a wood mill then used for grinding dye stuff, but formerly a fulling mill. All these mills were later to belong to Francis Yerbury of Belcombe Brook.

These years 1629 to 1640 were the period of King Charles' personal rule, in which he governed without summoning a parliament, leading to recurrent trouble particularly about taxation. Charles' extension of the liability to pay the Ship Money from the sea ports to inland tax payers as well was but one of a number of his actions that caused the riots recorded in many parts of Wiltshire as elsewhere. The country was split, too, in religious beliefs – even before 1604 it is said that puritan conventicles had been formed at Bradford and Broughton Gifford. And the cloth industry had not recovered from the disastrous Cockayne scheme in the previous reign which had virtually destroyed the valuable exports, particularly of all white, that is undyed, cloth.[20]

In the resulting divisions of loyalty, Michael Tidcombe, a royalist, was deeply involved. He became mayor of Devizes in 1643 and when the king intended to prosecute some of the parliamentary leaders, the earls of Pembroke, Salisbury and Northumberland, in the Assize court at Salisbury, Tidcombe was one of the lawyers employed to draw up the charges against them. Given the divided opinions of the times, the case came to nothing. But the parliamentarians did not forget Tidcombe's part in it, nor that he had been a receiver of contributions for the king's army. As a result he, like other royalists, was required to take a 'negative oath' of allegiance to parliament and pay a fine levied on his estates. He was arrested on the 11th November 1645 [21]; but complained that 'he had intended the night before his arrest to go to London to take the oath' and brought witnesses to prove it, though he did not say what had prevented him from going. On September 3rd in the next year he was still in custody and had appealed again to Parliament, saying that he had now taken the oath twice, in London and Devizes, that he had a wife and seven children, and debts amounting to £400. A fine of £217 was set, but when he appealed against it in 1647 it was increased to £450, 'he being an attorney.' And by June 1648 his lands were sequestrated for non-payment.

Eventually Tidcombe's property was returned. He retired to live quietly at Ashley and died there in 1662. There is a monument to him on the north wall in Bradford church. We noted that Great Ashley was his wife's property, left to her by her father John Blanchard, and by her to her son Edward. So as one might expect, Michael Tidcombe's will, at the P.R.O. lists just his various other farms, a very considerable estate, the bulk of which he left to William, the son of his second wife Rebecca.[22] The will was witnessed by two of his tenants, Thomas Baker from Turleigh, who made his mark, and Richard Nutt who signed in a good clear hand. It looks as if Little Ashley was in hand and was probably where Michael himself had been living. The will reveals the curious way in which holdings nominally of the same number of Yardlands sometimes differed appreciably in their acreages. For instance Tidcombe's tenants William Druce and Thomas Baker each occupied 1½ yardlands, yet there were 77½ acres in Druce's farm but only 62 in Baker's.

William Tidcombe's will is almost an exact copy of his father's in its description of the estate which he was leaving to his wife Elizabeth. He died in 1682. As was not unusual in those days, he had two brothers both called Michael. The elder of these Michaels had died in 1658. He and his wife have a memorial tablet, now apparently removed, under the arch between Winsley church tower and the nave of the present church, but this was said to have been originally inside the old church. The younger son Michael[II] inherited Haugh Farm from his brother William.

This Michael was married in 1674 to Sibyl Cooper, of a Trowbridge family of clothiers. He was a mercer with a shop, probably at Haugh, though perhaps it was in Bradford. He made his will at Christmas 1684, leaving £100 to each of his sons at 21, a silver tankard to the elder and a silver bowl to the younger. An inventory of his shop goods[23] gives a picture of some confusion with many remnants. Fabrics mentioned included linen, calico, fustian, buckram, linsey, ticking, muslin, cambric, holland, sarsnet, serge and swanskin. He had a large stock of buttons, 30 gross ordinary and 13 gross gimp (braid), 89 pairs of hose and 10 pairs of bodices. Trimmings included gold and silver golom (galloon, lace), silver, green silk, black and copper lace, and floral ribbon. He did not confine himself to dress requirements, but also stocked spices, raisins and currants, vinegar, metheglin, honey, tobacco, soap, hops, earthenware, besoms and glasses. The property passed to his wife Sibyl, and she appears in the Poor Rate books, paying rates on Haugh Farm until 1721.[24] In 1700 her eldest son, Michael[III], then aged 23, had married Mary Brodrip 21; their licence was for a wedding in Wells Cathedral.[25] And in their marriage settlement, completed a year later; Mary's portion was £250, and Haugh Farm was settled on her too.[26] They had two children, John and Mary.

By 1722, money was evidently a problem, for Michael, Mary and John together had to mortgage much of their land.[27] Michael was described as a clothier and John a shopkeeper (which could, however, mean a weaving or work shop), both of Haugh. The following year they sold five acres of land to Edward Thresher, who was then about to buy Winsley manor. The Haugh sale

died in 1552, but his son Antony still held the lease in 1581, when the Dean was persuaded to assign its remaining years to the Queen. Three months later she in turn assigned it to Sir Francis Walsingham, and he transferred its reversion to his daughter Frances. The Bristol records preserve a number of the manorial court books of this period, for the later 1590s and also for some of the 1620s. In the earlier books they are called courts of Edward Longe, farmer of the manor, with John Kent his Steward.[36] How, I wonder, does this fit in with Frances' lease? This Edward Longe (died 1622) was head of the branch of the Long family at Monkton near Broughton Gifford, ancestor of the Longs of Rood Ashton. The later courts, in the 1620s, were held by Edward's son John Long. While Edward was still alive, John was 'of Haugh', living at Parsonage Farm, but when Edward died, John succeeded him at Monkton and Thomas his son at Winsley Parsonage. The next we know is that, probably in 1645, at the end of the ninety nine years term of the original lease of the Rectory, the Dean and Chapter, granted a new one to 'John Long of Haugh'.

Let us take a look now at the lands belonging to this Rectory Manor. The 1562 Curia Recognitionis[37] gave some idea of the holdings in the manor, but for a fuller account we have to wait for later surveys. The earlier Court record names the tenants of the half dozen or so parsonage holdings in Winsley, but we are as usual left guessing what these farms were like or where they lay. Probably the reason for this was the scattered nature of the small fields (closes) then forming the farms. Even the tenant of Parsonage Farm, the chief of these holdings, cannot be identified with certainty from the court's descriptions. As we saw, the oldest surviving parts of the farmhouse, the lower floors of its high south end, were, to judge by their thick, 36 inch walls, built perhaps in the 14th century or before.[38] A major extension to the north with 20 inch walls and with hollow chamfered mouldings round its windows must have been put up in this latter part of the 16th century or shortly after; such a major building programme must have had a wealthy builder. The recognition court's roll names one man, Richard Wyllowes (or perhaps Willis) who may have been there. Richard Wyllys was prosperous, one of only three Winsley men who had to pay the 1545 Benevolence tax, and again, in the rental of the 1570s[39], Jane Willys, probably his widow, was assessed to pay much the largest rent of the customary rents to the manor. The recognition roll classifies Richard as holding land 'by indenture', effectively a sort of freehold, one up on the mere customary copyholdings. All in all, he sounds an interesting character, a likely candidate for the tenancy of the Parsonage Farm at this time. In fact in 1538 Wyllowes did indeed get a grant by an indenture from the Bristol Dean and Chapter, giving him, to quote the Latin, 'Crist ' of the Rectory of Haugh (Hawght in the original). The word Crist, a ridge or crest in the Latin, doesn't seem to make sense in the context. Possibly, however, we are misreading something like Cresse or Crisse, which Latham's Medieval Latin Word book says was used in the 17th century for an unusual kind of copyhold.[40] Hopefully, this is definite enough to make it reasonably sure that Wyllowes acquired Parsonage Farm and Haugh with its meadows, pastures, rights of common pasture and some woodland belonging to the Rectory.

Heading the list of Customary copyholders at Winsley in the minutes of the Curia Recognitionis was James Barnes, Drewe Druce's neighbour, who had two fairly large tenements in Turleigh on the Turleigh Manor site – and also a half-virgate holding in Winsley itself.[41] Barnes' copyhold had to be updated in 1570, probably after his wife died. Richard Dicke was next to acquire it, at a court in 1612, and in 1614 it was passed on into the hands of Dicke's sons John and George. In 1629, Richard Dicke junior was evidently living at a house in Turleigh, for he was reported by the jury at the Rectory court for cutting down eight oak trees in a close on his land without licence and selling them off for timber. The court states that the penalty for this was the forfeiture of the tenancy, but it does not seem as if this was carried out. In later deeds, Dicke's Turleigh land included several closes named Oakway beside the main Bradford road. Is this where he felled those oak trees?

The only farm for which the recognition court's survey gives us a list of fields and closes (and a translation is in the Notes) was held by Anna Wilshere, William's widow. One can recognise about half of their names, sufficient to attempt a map of these small, two or three acre pieces of land, scattered over the whole tithing. Gelestyche is obviously Kelstich, on the west side of the Conkwell lane just north of Church Farm; Wurnygshclose must be Warnage Close near the Dundas Aqueduct and Norwoods is at the corner of the lane near Haugh Farm. Rowweyes (Rowas) and Okeweys do not set a problem, but Elkeboriugh (or Eweborough) is unknown. Instinct suggests that the 2 acres called Styleclose was then only part of a much larger field of the same name.[42] Anna Wilshere's two acres close has since become Parson's Hurns, (that would be Parsonage Hurns), a rectory close out near Haugh Potticks. 'Hurns' is Erne's, an erne being a dwelling, as at Colerne and Potterne. Brodecroft looks like a three acre piece of land next to the larger Broadcroft on the north side of Conkwell Lane opposite Parsonage Farm, but Bradleys Mede has, I think, become Brawles (Broad Leys) down by the river near Belcombe Court. On the other hand, it may perhaps have become Huntley's Lease, now Hunter's Leaze, for Anna Willshere's farm became John Huntley's shortly after this? What the list does not say is where Anna's dwelling was.

There were two other Winsley prebendal holdings in 1563. David Atkyns' unidentified farmhouse with half a virgate somewhere at Haugh had been the family home since around 1550. And about the other, Guydyng's very small living, there is nothing to add here.

At the end of the Civil War the cathedral chapters were abolished and in 1649 a Parliamentary survey[43] was made, preparatory to selling off of the Bradford Rectory, the majority of this in Winsley. Here we find much more detailed descriptions of the farms. They are clearly the same ones as in the earlier court list. John Long had the Parsonage House at Haugh with its 100 acre of land. John Huntley at Ann Wilshere's farm had 45 acres, William Guiding only five, John Dike at Turleigh 49 acres and Edward Tidcombe 33 acres over near Sterts Lane and Great Ashley.

In 1652 all this rectory estate was in the hands of the Commonwealth Commissioners for the Sale of Church Lands and was bought by a Londoner, William Menheire. Shortly afterwards Menheire – would we call him an estate agent? – sold it to Sir Walter Strickland, who already shared the lordship of the lay Manor of Bradford with two other gentlemen. [44]

John Long died early in 1652/3. As we saw, his widow Anne came of a different branch of the family, the Longs of South Wraxall, and besides Upper Haugh Farm, John left her his interest in 'the Rectorie ... of Bradford', with its parsonages in all the Bradford tithings. The parsonage house of Winsley – namely Parsonage Farm – was then occupied by John's son Thomas and one William Woodley; one imagines that Woodley was manager or steward of Parsonage Farm. Anne outlived her husband by twenty years. In her will, among many bequests, she left money towards the repair of Winsley chapel. She also left 20 shillings to her cousin William Kiftill[45], the curate here, for preaching her funeral sermon. It had better be a good one at that price! Her daughter Mary, the wife of Hope Long of South Wraxall was to be her chief heir, so that Upper Haugh became the property of that Long family for almost the next two hundred years.

At the restoration of Charles II the Dean and Chapter recovered the Bradford Rectory. Presumably the lease to the Longs was reinstated soon after, for about 1667 Hope Long was granted a 21 year lease[46] of the rectory. It was duly renewed for a further term when it expired in 1688, but in 1693/4, only six years later, Long must have been in financial trouble for he mortgaged the Rectory in two parts to one John Mereweather for £1800. This still not proving enough to solve his problems, Long made a lengthy agreement[47] with John Hall, the then holder of Hall's manor at Bradford. Long was to surrender his lease to the Dean and Chapter of Bristol, and they were to be asked to grant a new 21-year lease, transferring the whole Rectory from Long to Hall. Of Hope Long's subsequent career, we only know that he was still alive until at least 1711, reaching a good old age. The agreement goes on to require that within one month of the making of the new lease, Hall was to grant a sub lease of the parsonage of Atworth and Wraxall to John Long – of Wraxall, no doubt – and another confirming the parsonage of Stoke to Richard Dicke, who already had the Manor of Limpley Stoke and the cloth mill there, a goodly estate. Nevertheless in spite of leasing out these parts of the Rectory, Hall was still unable to pay the main purchase money to Long. More had to be raised, and John Curl of Turleigh was persuaded to pay £2287 to Hope Long, receiving in return a lease of 'the Gleabe lands and Tythes lying within the Borough of Bradford and tythings of Great Winsley and Holt, except the prebendary manor'. This must surely be the only time our village aspired to the title of Great Winsley! All this sub letting enabled Hall to pay the purchase price to the Dean and Chapter, so setting up a scheme of subdivisions of the Rectory which was to continue until the Dean and Chapter finally sold all the prebendal land nearly 200 years later.

Let us now return to the Winsley part of the rectory, which John Curll or Curle was now taking over. He was the son of John Curll the elder, a Freshford clothier married to Sarah, daughter of Henry Davison,[48] the head of that substantial dynasty of Freshford clothiers, owners of the mill there. We have not been able to find out if these Freshford Curlls were related to the Walter Curle D.D. (1575 – 1647), Bishop of Winchester, a prominent supporter of Archbishop Laud in the 1640s, who played a leading part in the defence of the town for the king in the civil war.[49]

Our John Curll married Querina, daughter of John Gay of South Stoke near Bath, and it is interesting that Querina's memorial tablet in Bradford church records not only her own death in 1678 but that of her infant son Walter (1675 -1677) as well – was he perhaps named after the bishop?

In 1668, the Marquis of Winchester, Lord of Bradford Manor, leased the Church House in the town[50] to John Curll, with the important water supply there. This must have been the old church house, now the church hall. Curll's marriage must have been about that time, for when in 1670 Curll made a marriage settlement, giving the house to this wife, their first two children, their son Gay and daughter Elizabeth, were old enough to be the second and third lives in the copyhold.

The Curll connection with Winsley begins about this time; we read in 'another deed' :[51]

On the 10th November 1670, Querina wife of John Curll took a messuage, one *** of land and a messuage and a half *** of land in Turlin, both lately in the tenure of George Dicke, deceased, (the blanks, perhaps standing for 'virgate', are in the original). She also took a third farm whose the land was mostly in Winsley.'

These are the three properties which had belonged to James Barnes long before. Known by Curll's time as The Three Copyholds, they were in the part of the Rectory that was granted to John Curll under the agreement with John Hall.

The acreage of Querina's 2½ virgates of land in Turleigh agrees well with the 63 acres of this Turleigh estate in the Parliamentary survey. There were evidently two houses – two of the copyholds – on the land where Turleigh Manor now is, and the third was somewhere up in Winsley. The Curlls must soon have started on a large building programme at Turleigh. According to the W.B.R. report of our inspection of the house, Box stone was used, making it probable that the work was started by Richard Broad who had the quarry there and later moved to Winsley. He also carried out (not altogether satisfactorily, it seems) much of the stonework at the building of Dyrham House.[52] Richard settled in to Turleigh, where he presumably built the Broad family home, Uplands.

Except on the north face, the Turleigh House we now see is mostly in an 18th century style. The north side, however, is of coursed rubble without a plinth, whereas there is squared rubble on the west and south faces. With several of its windows of the older style the north remains probably Curll's work and it looks very much as if the rest of Curll's new house was largely refaced in the 18th century. This new and impressive house naturally became the residence of the successive holders of the Winsley section of the Rectory, whereas Haugh Parsonage Farm, which until John Long's time had been its principal house, now came to be occupied by a succession of tenant farmers.

John Curll had an important place in Wiltshire life, rising to the office of High Sheriff of Wiltshire in 1699. And in 1707 he died. As well as his Bradford and Freshford property, Curll had property in the village of Chirton near Devizes

Turleigh Old Rectory, now called Turleigh Manor. Built c.1700 on the site of two much old rectory farms

Turleigh Manor as it was until recently.

and in his will[53] he assigned the income from this to set up a number of charities. He appointed trustees for annual donations to be made to the Minister of Chirton, the Vicar of Bradford and the Rector of Freshford for the poor of their parishes. The Vicar of Bradford was ' to receive and distribute the sum of Thirty pounds to an hundred and twenty of such persons of the borough of Bradford and the Tithing of Winsley Leigh and Woolley... , who have or shall live by their honest labour, as the Vicar shall nominate and appoint, that is to say Five shillings a-piece to every of the 120 persons.' In 1889, as we read in the later edition of Canon Jones' 'Bradford on Avon', the Charity still paid out £16. 18s each year in strict accordance with Curll's instructions, but towards the end of the last century it was no longer possible to find eligible recipients. The income from Curll's gift now being of extremely small value, it remains dormant, its future undecided.

After John Curll's death, his lease of the Winsley Parsonage passed to his daughter Ann, by then the wife of Charles Dawe of Charlton Horethorne near Wincanton in Somerset. Charles Dawe is never described as 'of Turley', so presumably they never lived there, but their son John certainly did so.

The Dawe family's affairs were rather tangled[54] and were made worse by their difficulty in raising the cash to pay out some of John Curle's bequests. Chaos was added to the situation when, after the deaths of Charles and Ann, his brother Thomas took over the property but died intestate. Then, in the midst of a case in Chancey to sort out the ownership of Thomas's various properties, Ann's son John Dawe started negotiations to convey the lease of the Winsley property to Edward Thresher. All this was all brought to a halt on Thresher's death. A fresh legal start had to be made by means of a 'Bill ad Revivendum', involving the Lord Chancellor, to revive the case. Eventually the lawyers appointed John Thresher to be his father's executor, the sale of the Winsley rectory to John Thresher went through, and – wait for it – Thresher promptly sub-let the Winsley part of the property back to Dawe. And Dawe in turn seems to have mortgaged it to Joseph Baskerville, a clothier of Woolley Grange – and it had all taken twenty years and more to sort out. In this deed[55] the description of the estate is

> All that messuage or tenement at Turly late in the possession of John Curll deceased, and now of John Daw, and a close of pasture called the Hill adjoining (on the hillside behind Turleigh House), and all that messuage or tenement thereto adjoining now in the tenure of Henry Rudman as tenant to John Daw at Turlyn ... and all houses outhouses Dyehouses Stables outbuildings gardens ... Pools .etc...

and so on. As often happens in leases of this time, Dawe had to hire many of the house fittings from Baskerville. The lease requires him to undertake before the commencement of the Term (of the lease)

> .. to put the (houses) ... with the Glass, Windows Locks and Keys thereof ... in good tenantable Repair and so to keep the same (the said Glass Windows Locks and Keys only excepted) during the said Term.

It was quite common for clothiers to have dyehouses on their premises. Probably (my guess!) Dawe's dyehouse was near the Trows, just outside his front garden. When Joseph Baskerville's lease expired, the property was advertised in the Bath Journal :-

July 27th 1747. To be Lett
A very compleat well built House, with all necessary and convenient Out-Houses, Dye House, Wooll lofts, Stable, Orchard and Garden, well planted, situate at Turlyne, about four miles from Bath and two from Bradford, Wilts, and fit for a Gentleman or Tradesman: for Particulars, enquire of Mr Clutterbuck.

By 1766 the tenant was another clothier, Scudamore Perry, renting the property for £25 p.a. Perry was followed by Richard Atwood, yet another Bradford clothier, a friend of the politician Edmund Burke, who visited him at Turley on several occasions. During Atwood's time there, the Thresher accounts[56] frequently tell of more repairs carried out, for instance in July 1786,

Mending the Olde tyling at the house Plastering in garrett	£2 .. 3 .. 11½
Tyling the Dyhouse at Mr Atwoods	18 .. 0
For Halling 3 load of Tile	1.. 4.. 0

And inOct 1786 Work done at Mr Atwood Esquire

Taking up of the parler floore, working the ould Boord and laying the whole flore	13 .. 6

The issue of the *Bath Chronicle* of Tuesday, April 19th 1806 reported his death: 'Thursday, died at Turley, near this city, Richard Atwood, Esq., a character of most inestimable value; piety, integrity and benevolence were exemplified in all his words and activities'. His widow Anne, the daughter of a Trowbridge clothier, — Cox; outlived him by more than thirty years.

Meanwhile, the lease of the whole Bradford Rectory from the Dean and Chapter had also expired in 1785. It had long been in the hands of the Duke of Kingston who had inherited it, like the Hall in Bradford, from his ancestor John Hall. Seeking a new lessee to succeed him the Duke, the Dean and Chapter issued a short valuation of the various 'properties to be disposed of'. Of these, The Three Copyholds, at £70..5s..6d, was easily the most valuable.[57]

After John Thresher bought the Winsley portion of the Rectory from John Dawe, his family held it for nearly a century. He left it to his widow Ellen, and after her death in 1753 it was held by Dame Ellen Wrey, John Thresher's eldest daughter. Several letters, preserved among the Bristol records[58], show her tenure was a time of periodical but often acrimonious strife about rent increases which the Dean was trying to impose on the Rectory tenants. There is also an interesting note among these papers about the travelling arrangements made for a visit by a party from the Dean to the chapter's various properties around Bradford. Ellen Wrey retained her lease of the property till 1811, and, Richard Atwood having died in 1808, it was to his widow Ann that the fresh lease was granted.

Richard Atwood's name was commemorated in the name of another interesting Victorian. Sir Richard Atwood Glass (1820 – 1873),[59] born in Winsley, became well known as a pioneer manufacturer and builder of telegraph cables. He constructed the first submarine cable, from Dover to Calais, about 1852, and under his direct supervision his company laid the first transatlantic cables. After the failure of his first attempt in 1865, an improved cable succeeded in the following year; it had a long and useful life.

Soon after being granted the Rectory, Ann Atwood obtained a licence for a Dissenter's place of worship at a building belonging to Turleigh House.[60] This small Baptist congregation survived for some sixty years and, quoting from the Women's Institute scrapbook, 'It is said that when all the congregation had arrived at the chapel, her ladyship would enter, followed by her butler carrying a prayer book on a velvet cushion. Then everyone stood, while she went to her pew; when she was seated, she motioned to them to sit down. After the service, all the people remained in their seats till Lady Atwood (was the W.I. really authorised to promote her to this rank?) had left the chapel.' In her will in 1842, Ann Atwood, then at the age of 94, left all her Parsonage property to trustees, and finally in 1861 the Dean and Chapter sold all their Winsley property, so the rectory manor, by then an anachronism, ceased to exist.

It remains to add a few words about the later history of the Haugh Parsonage Farm, the largest in the rectory. In the later 18th century when the Thresher property was shared out between John's four daughters, Parsonage Farm was held by Dionysia and her tenants. Abel Moxham was her tenant there for a number of years, and from his lease one gathers that Dionysia kept a rather firm hold on her tenant's activities.[61] Moxham was leasing several of the rectory farms, a total of 171 acres, among them Church farm (called Winsley Farm in those days) as well as Parsonage Farm. Dionysia retained for herself the quarries in Conkwell Woods and 'the liberties of Hunting, Fishing and Fowling', and laid down detailed conditions for his tenancy. Moxham was to cultivate the arable land in a husbandlike way. He must not plough more than two thirds of this land in any year – the remaining third part to be 'summer Fallowed and lye with clover or with Tyrnips or Vatches so as such Vatches are either fed off with sheep (that probably means grazed by Dionysia's sheep) or mown for hay and not gathered for seed. Moreover Moxham was to 'carry forth and lay abroad in a husbandlike manner all the Haystraw, Dung and soil that shall be made upon the same premises shall be used upon the same premises and not elsewhere'. He had of course to keep all the 'mounds, Bounds, Gates, Fails and Fences' in repair and to pay....the window tax and House tax and perform the Service and Labour to the Highway. And so on...and so on...and so on... One the other hand Dionysia was to pay all other dues and keep all the buildings and walls in good repair and to allow Moxham to take rough timber for 'plough Boot' – that sounds medieval! – and have 4 hundred(weight?) of faggot wood for firewood.

In 1766 the farm was the scene of a violent incident. For some time there had been unrest among the weavers of Bradford, whose wages had been reduced. The price of corn had risen, too, and some farmers had contributed to the rise by reserving their grain for whisky. There was genuine hardship among the weavers, who started rioting. Two companies of soldiers were sent to Trowbridge to quell the riots. In September there was serious trouble in Bradford; food and some clothing was taken, and a number of farms were attacked. A coroner's inquest held on the 23rd September that year [62] recorded

About 11 p.m. on the 20th September a great number assembled riotously at Haugh (Parsonage) Farm, Abel Moxham's dwelling house, and tried to break and enter it; in the attempt William Sainsbury was shot and killed.

The verdict was justifiable homicide by a person or persons unknown. The *Bath Chronicle* for the 9th October adds a little detail:

On Thursday, John Hinton of Bradford, broadcloth weaver, was committed to Salisbury gaol, for assembling with a riotous mob, 20th September last, and attempting, with a candle, to set fire to the ricks of Abel Moxham near that place.

7
Burghope and Winsley House

W INSLEY'S parish registers survive only from the 18th century onwards, the earliest entitled 'A new Register Book of Winsley beginning in the year of our Lord God 1724 '. From then on we possess an almost complete run of them. The 1724 book must surely once have had a predecessor. In fact even now all is not lost from the previous years, for in 1597 it was decreed that after each year's end at Easter,[1] every church was to make a fair copy of the past year's entries. Known as the Bishop's Transcript, this was to be sent to the Diocesan registry, in Winsley's case at Salisbury, and many of them survive. The handwriting of the Winsley transcripts shows that as often as not it was one of the churchwardens who wrote the copy, the curate only adding his signature to theirs. In most years, even as far back as Charles I's reign, at least one of our two churchwardens could sign his name – not a bad record for a small village! These transcripts therefore preserve the names of our curates, as well as many of the 17th century parish registers, apart, that is, for a gap in the Commonwealth years.[2] When the transcripts were resumed at the restoration in 1660, it took a few years for the system to get back into its stride. The transcripts for 1661, 62 and 63 were all combined into a single document by the curate William Kiftill with the help of the wardens John Wilshere (it was in his handwriting) and John Dicke. There are very few entries in these years – they were perhaps being compiled from memory! Later, there was another, unexplained, gap between Kiftill's last signature in 1680 and James Butter's first in 1693. Butter had been curate since about 1688, but in 1694 he was appointed rector of Ditteridge near Box as well, while still remaining our absentee curate. Another long interval without transcripts follows Butter's death, after which the proper registers began. During his time at Ditteridge, Butter expected the people of Winsley to go over to him at Ditteridge church for their weddings and funerals. The Ditteridge registers do contain the entries for a number of Winsley marriages in these years;[3] still others are to be found in the Bradford registers.

More information for these early years is to be found in the records of the periodic visitations which the Archdeacons of Salisbury used to make around the diocese. For these occasions the local church wardens prepared statements called 'Churchwardens' Presentments' of their replies to schedules of questions regarding their church. On the 11th September 1674, for instance, they, John Wilshere, 'the elder', who could write, and John A-Court, who apparently could not, went over to Devizes to one of these visitation meetings. In their replies to the questions in the schedule, the word 'presentable' was often used with rather a different meaning from its present one. Thus in Part 1 of their report,[4] the church wardens state that 'on the Churches, Chappells, and the furniture and ornaments thereunto belonging: we find nothing presentable'. It means, not that all these matters were in urgent need of repair, but that everything was in good order – there were no shortcomings to report. In Part 2, their report on the churchyard, houses, glebe, and in Part 3, the Ministers, too, 'we find nothing presentable'. On the parishioners, however, their report was that 'wee present John Dagger and his wife for not paying the Vicar his dues. Otherwise nothing presentable'. In another Presentment in 1683, the picture is perhaps not quite so good: 'Imprimis, wee present two of our Common prayer Books belonging to our church are torn and decayed and wee desire time till Christmas to provide new ones or to mend ye same.' and 'Item wee present that John Druce dyed in our parish in or about May last past'. But by 1698 'All things in order in our parish', though the Bradford wardens said 'We present John Clark ... our chirurgeon ... and Thomas Bush Schoolmaster for practising as we understand without Licence'. As we might expect, unlicensed midwives were presented on several occasions. These presentments give regular reports, too, on other church affairs. In 1662, shortly after the Commonwealth period, the church and its ornaments were out of repair. Erring villagers were routinely reported for not attending church or not having their children baptised – all very presentable, no doubt! On the other hand, the churchwardens state with pride that the baptismal register contains the mother's name as well as the father's. There are notes of improvements to the church, too. Thus in 1788 'the Church was new pued and pulpit', and in 1780 'the Bell was put upun the tower' – the small striking bell of a new clock, housed in a little turret, visible in many old photographs.

Curates in those days were often called on to act as witnesses to the wills of their parishioners, many of whom would be illiterate; perhaps partly for this reason, in most wills from Tudor times onward it was the custom to make some bequest to the church and often, in earlier years, to Salisbury cathedral as well. So in 1547 William Wylshyre left 'to the Churche of Wynesley one

To conclude the story of our Burghope, I am very grateful to Pamela Slocombe for bringing together the many stages in the growth of the house.[10]

Phase 1 A cruck-built house with timber framed walls. Three room and cross passage plan with a two-bay open hall. The apex of a truss here is of a type with no currently known parallels but is related to 14th century types and is probably an early example. [It has since been shown by dendro dating that the tree for this truss was felled in the summer of 1317].

Phase 2 The walls converted to stone. Fireplace constructed within the hall creating a wide cross passage behind it with a new stone outside porch. House still single storey. Late 15th century. A parallel with the fireplace from Ilminster, Somerset, dating from c.1480.

Phase 3 Protestant black letter inscription put over hall fireplace. c.1540.

Phase 4. The hall and parlour ceiled over with ovolo moulded gable dormer windows lighting the first floor rooms. Structure of W. room (originally kitchen) rebuilt. Late 16th – early 17th century.

Phase 5 W. room altered to parlour and a new kitchen added behind the east end of the house, shallow hollow moulded windows, alterations to roof. c. 1690.

Phase 6. Ground floor doorway to W. end from entrance hall. Stable block? 18th c.

Phase 7. Gothick fireplace at W end room; re-used church windows inserted in W. end wall, c.1841.

Phase 8 Alterations and service wing added by Miss Hope-Johnstone, c.1881.

It is said there is a cellar with a well in it under part of this house. Rumour also has it that there was once an underground tunnel or two running from the cellar to the manor house and or to the cellar at Scarth.

Pam Slocombe's W. B. R. report links the history of the house tentatively to the church and the curates. The original house with its two bay open hall might have been a yeoman's farmhouse but its subsequent alterations in the 15th century (massive early fireplace, porch and stone walls) suggests a higher status though not quite that of a manor. It could have been the house of a freeholder but it suits even more for it to have been a parsonage. Its relative nearness to the church and its subsequent link to the curates in the Redman family give some justification for this theory. If this is correct then the Abbess of Shaftesbury Abbey was the original builder.

Winsley House

APPROACHING WINSLEY from Bath along the old main road into the village one first passes Burghope and the crossroads at the Wheatsheaf corner. The road then narrows, with Winsley Croft on the left and on the top of the wall, over a doorway on the right, the most prominent of three stone hounds

– Talbots, that is, for they all have heraldic chains round their necks. The wall was no doubt made to bulge out here, we may be sure, not for the dogs' peace of mind or just to obstruct the traffic, but because the doorway led to the old Winsley House, whose inhabitants thereby gained a bit more space between themselves and the road.

In James Fairbairn's *Book of Crests*, none of the families whose crests are Talbots appears to have any connection with Winsley, so the origin of our hounds is a mystery. Our other two hounds, standing on the gateposts on either side of the drive up to the house, have had a rough time in recent years. For firstly, sometime in the 1970s, they were stolen, then restored to the tops of their pillars, and shortly after smashed to pieces in a traffic accident. Fortunately the fragments were gathered up and stored, and have recently been used as models for a new

The hound on the wall outside Winsley (Dorothy) House

pair of hounds. So they are back in their proper places. Just over the gateway below the dog on the wall there is a stone bearing the date 1657 in what appears to be the correct style for the year. It must commemorate some event in the history of the house, but does not seem to relate to the hound.

The present Winsley House, now Dorothy House, was built in 1902 by a barrister, Arthur Morier Lee. What brought him to Winsley we do not know, but he was evidently captivated by the fine site. An inscription which he put on a gable of his new house bears a Latin quotation from Horace which may be translated 'That nook of earth's surface has a smile for me before all other lands.' [11] He must nevertheless have been a restless character, for he put his new house on the market in 1906. Apparently it did not sell, for Lee was still on the electoral roll till 1907. It had, however a series of owners and occupiers in the years leading up to the Great War. The W. I. Scrapbook tells a tale of village intrigue from those years, leading up to the building of the Village Hall in the years after that war. The Davies family, living at Winsley House from 1924, are remembered for their efforts towards the building of the Hall, a project proposed and strongly opposed in the years before the war.

The stone for the new Winsley House was quarried in Winsley and the stone roof tiles collected locally. The quarrying industry was in decline at the end of the nineteenth century, and the work on the house must have been welcome. Though the old house was completely taken down, a detached coach house and stables were retained. It stands at an angle to the new building line and is connected to it by a covered way.

In 1952 the Sutcliffe School, a remedial school for boys, came to Winsley from Bath. There were alterations to the house, and the school was formally opened in 1954 by Basil Henriques, the London magistrate. It closed in 1991, and in 1993 the Dorothy House Foundation, whose hospice then occupied a number of inconvenient Victorian houses in Bath, purchased the Winsley House site. More alterations and extensions followed, providing more suitable hospice premises. By 1995 their construction work was finished, and in June their staff and patients moved in.

The old Winsley House links together a number of interesting strands of Winsley's history. It was the head of an extensive farm, though, curiously, in the 17th century the house itself with a modest garden stood isolated among the fields of an even older, probably fifteenth century farm once called Cornelius's and now Winsley Croft. We have not been able to discover who James Cornelius was, though there seem to have been a number of related families. An Edward Cornelius was rector of Wingfield in the 1690s, and the name was more frequent around Mere in the south of the county.

Shortly before the old Winsley House was demolished, an article about a 'Picturesque Village Ramble' round Winsley appeared in the Bath and County Graphic, and in it is a photograph of the old house. Most of it is hidden by enormous yews trees on the lawn and the whole front is covered in creepers As far as one can tell, it was a long, rather lowish building, say of the first half of the seventeenth century, of a style earlier than the date 1657 on the stone below the dog would suggest. It stood end on to the road, to the west of the new house. The documented history goes back to a lease granted in 1713 by Elizabeth Kent, the lady of the manor, to her nieces Elizabeth and Maria Criswick, recording a previous lease to Thomas Baker of Turleigh in the 17th year of Charles II, which is 1667, shortly after the births of Baker's two eldest children John and Marion. It seems that the house previously belonged to Richard Dicke the Turleigh clothier. Baker had married his granddaughter Barbara Dicke. Richard lived – again probably – where Turleigh Grange now is and later generations of the Baker family continued to live there. At the end of the 1500s, Dicke bought a house and land in Winsley from James Barnes, Drewe Druce's neighbour in Turleigh, and possibly Barnes bought it from John Crynne. Could this have been Winsley House?

Returning to the 1713 lease, Elizabeth and Maria Criswick, daughters of the Bristol merchant Sir Henry Criswick and nieces of Elizabeth Kent of Winsley manor, probably never lived at the house, though for much of the next century it was to be known as Cressick's House. By 1702, Thomas and Barbara were dead and their daughter Marian had married William Gay (hence the house was alternatively known as Gay's Farm). According to the Pertikuler, the farm was a medium sized one of about 50 acres, valued at £20 p.a. A heriot, her best beast, would have been claimed by the manor when Barbara, then a widow, died in 1716. And the lease to the two Creswick ladies then came into effect. There is a memorial tablet to the Bakers on the face of the tower of Winsley church, but unfortunately it has become practically illegible during recent years.

The Creswicks were an important family of Merchant Venturers at Bristol. We read of one of their ships running short of beer and water on a voyage from La Rochelle and Cresicke in France. In 1653, too, Henry Creswicke was up before the Venturers' court because a ship of his, 'The Joseph of Bristol' was taken by the Dutch near Gibraltar, and in the same year the 'Fortune of Bristoll' was 'on her last voyadge from this Port toewards Croswick' (Croisic near St Nazaire in Brittany). It sounds as if the family name was derived from the French port. Their cargoes were often of wine; a record at The Hall, the court of the Merchant Venturers,[12] in 1664, tells how the merchants shared out the cargo of one such ship. This ship, belonging to Mr. Anthony Gay had arrived, and he announced to the Hall that he had on board Twenty and Five Pipes of Canary wine and 17 Buttes of Malliga being strangers wine, whereupon Sir Henry Creswck (and a number of others) were voted and ordered to treat and bargaine for the same. And to allot it (if they buy it) amongst the Company according to custom, And to meet to morrowe morming at Ten of the Clocke for the doeing thereof.

The lease to the two Creswick ladies mentions the house, with its garden, orchard, backside, barn, stable and outhouse as well as the land. Mistress Creswick paid rates on the farm from 1719 to 1727, but in the following year the rate book has 'Creswick or occupier', so maybe the farm had been sub-let. About this time the Winsley house farm passed from them into the hands of the Cottles. Moses Cottle had come to Winsley from Monkton Farleigh and Little Atworth, where his family was long established – and the house now the Stonar School used to be known as the ancient manor of Atworth Cottles. The family connection is medieval; Richard Cottle held it in 1242 [13]. Moses Cottle was born in 1677, and in 1701 he married Sarah, daughter of John Blatchley, of Upper Haugh farm. The marriage seems to have come rather late, for Moses junior was christened on his parents' wedding day.[14] Moses I followed the Blatchley family, living at Cornelius' farm, (The Croft) which was his home for several years. He built up a considerable estate of houses and land, among them the freehold of Winsley House, still called Gay's or Criswick's in his days. His property shows up prominently on the 1727 map.[15] He was, we remember, deeply involved in the building of the first bridge over the Avon at the bottom of Winsley Hill with the toll house at the far end of the bridge.

His son Moses II, however, did live in Winsley House and received a visit there from John Wesley, who had recently experienced the conversion which changed his life, and had come to work amongst the miners of Kingswood. Wesley made the first of many visits to Bradford in July 1739, and on one of his early visits, probably in October of the same year, he wrote in his diary that leaving Bristol at 6 a.m., he had called at the house of Mr. Cottle in Winsley for 'prayer, singing, tea and conversation'.[16] It is very likely that Moses Cottle's brother in law Richard Baker, Thomas's great grandson, was also present at this gathering, and perhaps also his neighbour John Wiltshire who lived in Winsley at Scarth – or Rock House, to give it its former name. These men were later trustees of the earliest Methodist rooms at Bradford and Freshford, and when in 1808 a chapel was to be built in Winsley, it was John Wiltshire's son William[17] who gave a lease of part of the garden at Scarth for it at a peppercorn rent. The plot was large enough for a caretaker's house as well. The deed tells in detail the restrictions imposed on the use of the land as a chapel site. The lower half of the front wall of this small building can still be seen in the Drung, the lane next to the present chapel (called Jones's Lane in those days). An old photograph shows it was a typical small chapel of the period. With the opening of this Winsley chapel the membership rose rapidly from 12 to 22 or more.

It seems likely, too, that John Cottle from Monkton Farleigh, Moses's cousin, was also present at the meeting at Winsley House and it is fairly sure that the Winsley Methodists began as a group meeting at Farleigh in a loft over the stables attached to John Cottle's house next the 'Fox and Hounds' at Farley Wick. The deeds of that house provided that a room in the house was to be at the disposal of John Wesley or any of his preachers during their visits. On his deathbed, Cottle was visited by Wesley, who came specially to see 'that good old man'.

Moses Cottle junior did not marry until he was forty one. In the marriage settlement Moses's father was described as a yeoman, but the son called himself a gentleman. The criterion for moving up the social scale in those days was usually the amount of land a man possessed. Six children were born to them, but when the youngest was only a year old, his father died. In these difficult circumstances, Moses's widow Silvestra moved away from Winsley, first to Bath and then to Bitton, where her married sister lived.

This Moses Cottle had died in 1748, and three years later his Winsley property was bought by the brothers William and David Lea, then in the process of building up their large Winsley estate. Their grandfather William Grant of

Bradford, rough mason, had left land and five houses to his children at his death in 1714. He had perhaps been involved in a lot of the building above Newtown about this time. His daughter Susannah married John Lea of Sherston in 1690. He described himself as a drover. Eleven children were born of this marriage, of whom William and David were the second and third. They continued to prosper, for between 1744 and 1752 they bought six local farms round Bradford (Haugh and Upper Bearfield, Frankleigh House, part of France Farm and of course the Croft and Winsley House) besides some cottages. When, later, they decided to divide their estate between them, Winsley House was in William's share. Their lengthy deed of settlement provides an excellent schedule of all the various fields and closes as they had become soon after John Thresher had finished reorganising the old strip fields into the larger and more manageable ones.

Richard Lea, the elder brother of William and David, had a daughter Anne who married a John Jones of Frankley, of a family of Bradford apothecaries. They seem to have had a definite connection with Winsley, for he or a namesake of his had a large tomb in Winsley churchyard. It was, according to the W.I. book, an impressive structure with a large carved urn on a plinth, and a large canopy over it. It goes on to say: –

Jones died in 1754; the funeral procession must have traversed the narrow winding lane (from Frankley) to Winsley. Two persons known to present villagers (once) met the procession when returning home in the small hours of the morning. One was the district nurse of the day returning from a maternity case, the other was the much respected schoolmistress of the village school. The first realised at once the uncanny nature of the apparitions and was terrified; the other thought nothing of it except that it was an odd time to have a funeral.

This John, a naval surgeon, served at Falmouth and was often at sea in revenue cutters during the French

The monument of John Jones of Frankley, who died in 1754. It was deemed unsafe and demolished recently.

wars of the mid century. A letter which his wife wrote to a cousin at Frankleigh is worth quoting.

Falmouth, April; ye 21st, 1762
Dear Coz[n] Stevens·
Mr Jones's stay at home was so short yt he had not time to settle any of his Business – therefore tis all left to me, and this is to desire of you to let me know what cash you have got of ours in your Hands and to remit ye same to Mr John Yerbury [– and more money details follow – and then.. –] please to give my love to your wife and tell her I intend writing to her soon – should have done it before – but many things has prevented me, indeed I was in great expectations of being in Bradford this sumer – but it could not be – but hope nothing will prevent us from keeping a joyful Xmas together – Mr Jones has got a promise from Secretary Potts yt he will get him leave to stay home next voyage – so yt I am almost assured of it. I wish you could see my Dear Boy I know you would like him – he is a litle slim (?) fellow very tall of his age but slim – your Nancy immagine is a great girl by this time – not quite so talkative as her mother – excuse me Mrs Stevens – I was in some hopes last summer yt I might see you here – but I have dropt all thoughts of having yt pleasure now – but I beg you will not come to Plymouth without coming to see me, tis but a days Journey – & sure you can ride yt to come & see me – or I shall think it very bad & unkind – I hope you and your family continue well, with our Friends at Stoke I beg my love to all & my Duty to Uncles and Aunts – I wish you would tell Aunt B. Lea yt I will write her soon, I want much to see her. I pray god to preserve her life – I remain Dear Cos[n]
Yours most affectionately
Ann Jones

And a letter (1760) from John Jones: –

Hope some business will call you to Plymouth & then of consequence you must reach Falmouth or Nancy would certainly declare war with you. My Pacquet is not yet arrived – I am almost afraid she never will as she will have been due these three weeks & there is so many French Privateers in our waters that it is almost impossible for a ship to escape them – if she should be taken I shall not leave England till April- ....[18]

Coming back to the Winsley part of the story, in 1764 William was the victim of a robbery. The indictment reads:

Thomas Dike committed Nov. 5th 1764 By John Bythesea Esq.[19] and charged with feloniously breaking and entering in to the Dwelling of William Lea of Bradford

Gent, and stealing takeing and carrying away Seven Silver Waistcoat buttons of the value of 2s and also three pair of Mourning Shoe Buckles of the value of 1s, which he hath confessed.

This was not Dike's only crime. After cloth had been woven, and fulled in a mill, it was hung on racks with tenter hooks to dry. A clothier, Scudamore Perry of Turleigh House, had had one of his cloths fulled and hung out, probably at Avoncliff Mill, and at the assizes, Dike was charged with vandalising it:

> Thomas Dike committed Nov 5th 1764 by John Bythesea and charged upon Oath with feloniously taking a light grey Spanish Broadcloth with a knife as the same was Hung on Tenters to dry in a close situate at Bradford in three Different places the property of Scudamore Perry of Bradford Clothier of the value of £20.

For these misdeeds Dike was sentenced to seven years transportation to America – this was before Australia was brought into use for that purpose. It seems probable that Dike returned to England after serving out his sentence.

A few years before this there was the case of a Winsley teenager, Mordecai Bollen, a labourer, hanged for robbery. He assaulted a man on the road from Bradford to Turleigh and stole 2s in silver and 9d in halfpennies. He was not recognised or caught, but two years later he was arrested upon suspicion of mugging a woman and robbing her of £3. He was about to be discharged for want of evidence when his first victim recognised him and pointed him out amongst a large throng of people in the court. He could not escape the gallows this time, and a picture

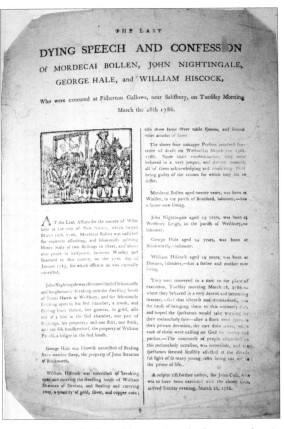

This is part of a broadsheet printed when Mordecai Bollen of Turleigh was hanged for robbery in 1786.

The 15th century church tower, the only surviving part of the old parish church.

of the hanging was printed on a broadsheet and circulated shortly afterwards, a supposed confession as an awful warning of his sad fate.

After 1805 the Lea empire began to be broken up. Up to this point it had become the second largest in Winsley, exceeded only by the manor, but now the house passed through the hands of various owners. Among them, it was briefly occupied from 1828 by the Rev. W. B. Cousins, the curate of Winsley.

The next owner of Winsley House was William Stone, a solicitor with a practice in Pippet Street (Market Street) in Bradford. He was much more influential in the life of the village than of Bradford. He was a son of William Stone, County treasurer for Somerset. William junior was Clerk to the magistrates. He and his wife Frances, or Fanny as she was known, had two sons and six daughters, but the family health seems to have been poor. Though most of the children survived their childhood, they died as young men and women. There is a family memorial in the parish church.

Like many of his predecessors at Winsley House, William Stone built up a good estate here. Among other property, he owned a rank of five cottages which once stood opposite the future site of the village hall, as well as many of the quarrymen's cottages in Murhill. He also had Murhill House, then called Murhill Cottage, and the famous strawberry gardens in Murhill, which flourished on the sunny south facing slopes there.

It is to his exertions that we owe the preservation of our ancient church tower. When in 1840 it was decided to build a new church at Winsley, it was at first proposed to take down the entire old building, including the 15th century tower. Stone fought to defend the tower, and won.[20] The actual rebuilding we will describe in the next chapter. However, when the rebuilding was complete, Stone instructed his gardener to dig up a number of yew trees from his grounds at Winsley House, and with the help of the curate they were replanted in the churchyard, where they still flourish.

Stone was also partly instrumental in bringing the railway to Bradford. Stations had been built along the proposed route, but it was then found that no funds remained to lay the track, 'to the extreme discontent of the inhabitants'. William threw himself into the cause, and after a delay of nine years, the line was opened.

In the 1871 Census, the residents were William Stone, his second wife, his daughter Sarah and son-in-law J.W. Stapleton, a general practitioner. There was a general servant and a cook. William died the next year, aged eighty five. Both his sons had died before him so the estate was sold by auction in Bradford Town Hall. Murhill House was also on offer, with 25 other cottages and plantations of larch and spruce.

This was followed by the sale of the contents of Winsley House, which sheds some light on the lives of the owners. They include Brussels and Turkey carpets, feather beds, Silver and plate, Guns, Rifle, Antique pistols and swords, rare old wines, 70 valuable old paintings, 50 engravings and prints, 300 books, a Sewing Machine by Wheeler and Wilson, a set of plate Harness, wheel chair, Brewing and Dairy utensils, and two court dressers.[21]

Winsley House did not sell at the auction, but was bought the next year for £2204, including 17 acres of land. The buyer was Captain Gibney, who evidently continued to work the quarry which is now under the Chase, from which he had a small railway track (not a 'sacred processional way', pace Guy Underwood's note in the W.I. Scrapbook) leading down to the canal for the transport of the stone; for this he paid a rent of £1 a year (note in Lot 26 in the sales particulars). Part of this can still be seen, a raised strip running diagonally across the field below. Gibney also intended to make changes to the house: The Wiltshire Times of the 14th March 1874 carries his advertisement for 'Builders disposed to Contract for the Carpenter's, Joiner's, Plumber's, Tiler's, Plasterer's, Painter's, and Glazier's work to be done in partly REBUILDING WINSLEY HOUSE,' the architect being Charles Adye of Bradford. It is probable that this work was never carried out, and in 1902 the old house was demolished.

8
Slaymakers and Quarrymen

I N T H E C O U R S E of Winsley's history, one of the most frequently occurring family names is Wilshere, though some others are not far behind. The name occurs in many village records hereabouts from the earliest times and we should therefore, I am sure, pursue their story a bit further. At Holt there was a Laurence Wilteshere among the taxpayers as far back as 1332, but at Winsley we have only traced the family back to Joan, Thomas and Henry Willshere who were in trouble as Lollards in Turleigh just before the reformation. Shortly after, Wylliam Wyltshyre wrote one of the oldest Winsley wills we have. That will was mainly concerned with a flock of twenty sheep which his elder son James was to look after until his younger brother was old enough to care for them. And we learn that William also owned a cottage in Freshford which he was leaving to his daughter Alys. He appointed seven neighbours, men whose names we met earlier, among them Druce Carter and Richard Meade, to be his overseers. About forty years later, in the rental of the 1570s[1], there were six Wilshere families of prosperous customary tenants, three of them called John. Some of these families can be traced through to the 18th century, when for instance we have already seen there was a John Willshere who married Richard Druce's daughter Elinor, and with her acquired Turleigh House. This John Wilshire was 'of Westwood', but his parents had earlier moved there from Turleigh.

In this chapter, however, we will try to reconstruct the story of another line, the descendants of John the son of Humffrey Wyllshyre of Wynnsleye, who died in 1574. Naturally, practically nothing is known about these earliest members of this family; their wills imply they were fairly well off, calling themselves husbandmen. In 1612, John's son James left a will (witnessed by Henry Redman the curate), with an inventory that shows he had a small but comfortable home by the standards of the day. The 'Hawle' looks sparsely furnished – we read only of a table and two forms, with 18 Powles[2] of pewter, a cubbord and 3 candlesticks – but there is much more in the kitchen and the chamber (a featherbed, two flock beds and the bedclothes). There was a buttery, and in a Lofte were two more bedsteads, 54 pounds of wool, a waybeam, scales and wayghtstones ‾ that is, stone weights: it is not so long ago that we weighed ourselves – and sacks of potatoes – in stones. There was 50 shillings worth of wheat in the barn. He had a good wagon and the farm was well stocked with animals, among them 5 oxen, 2 Kyne, a mare and her colt, and 7 pigs, as well as 52 sheep and lambs. This inventory was being taken at the end of June, and the crops were growing well – James had 10 good acres of wheat and 22 of barley in his fields.

In each of the next two generations, the head of the family was known as John the Elder, husbandman, of Winsley. Should we perhaps call them John the elder Elder and the younger Elder? One imagines they remained in the old family house, passed on as was usual from the father to his eldest son. The inventories taken with their wills in 1670 and 1686 respectively describe a growing house with several more rooms than the three James had[3], and also three upstairs chambers over them. In particular, there was a room with the distinctive title of the Street Chamber, implying that the house stood endwise-on to the road. The naming of these rooms must have been rather random, for in 1670 the Street Chamber had the brewing equipment in it – three barrells, three bottells, a brewing vatte, a Trendle, a Tub, two pails, a range (i.e. a special kind of sieve), a malt sieve, two other seeves, two horses (stands) for the barrells and so on, of total value £1. 10. 0 – surely this was a ground floor room. The Street Chamber in 1686 was quite different – in it there then were two bibles and other books, a bedstead, a small quantity of wool and a few more things of that sort. The barrells and the rest were downstairs in 'the room under the street chamber'. And with a bit of luck, a room name like this may be a clue for finding out where this house was – standing end-on to the road. The 1841 Tithe Map, made about 150 years later, is the oldest with enough detail for our purpose. It shows only three end-on houses in the village – and two of those, The Croft, on the main road, with another, the old Winsley House opposite it, were Moses Cottle's property, not Wilshire's. James Cornelius farmed at the Croft around 1700: clearly neither of these can ever have been the Wilshires' home. The third, Rock House, now called Scarth, lies just across the road from the Seven Stars. One may have doubts on its position, though, for its end-on room is shown further from the road than one would expect. So we need to find a firmer link between this house and the Wilshires' old farm.

Looking carefully at the building itself, there are many features that do suggest that Scarth could be the old Wilshire house. Starting as a single east-west row, it has had numerous stages of alteration and rebuilding. The eastern bays were the oldest – perhaps the Hall, Kitchen and Buttery that James

Willshere had in 1612. Most of their walls are 26 inches thick, and the rest up to 36 inches, not unusual for the 16th/early 17th century. And upstairs the lower halves of the walls are the same ones continued, but then, after a wide step half way up, the upper parts of the walls are much more recent and thinner. Clearly the house roof used to be much lower, with the old eaves line at the step. The western half of the house is younger, perhaps of the eighteenth century, with more recent additions and alterations. A feature of this end of the house is that starting under the westernmost room, a flight of steps, with a barrel rolling slope beside it, leads down to a cellar. This ends in a rough brick wall. So we may say the old half of Scarth could well have been the old Wilshire house – or at least of the same age.

Scarth certainly did belong to the later Wiltshires, for we saw that in 1808 the children of William Wiltshire, a descendant of John Wilshere the Elder, gave a plot in his garden at Scarth as site for the proposed Methodist chapel. And William's father John Wilshire the Slaymaker also lived there, paying the poor rates on it from 1721 onwards. He was the grandson of John Wilshere the Elder, but I still have doubts about who had the house in the years between.

In his will of 1686, old John Wilshere the second Elder left his house and the residue of his goods to his eldest son John, who died only three years after his father. The death appears to have been unexpected, for he made no will, and what happened next is uncertain. He does not seem to have left a widow to inherit the house. Old John's 1686 will seems to imply that his second son Robert had by then set up home on his own and was no longer living in the family home. This Robert, like his son John, was a slaymaker, and was probably making a good living, for his father left him only a token legacy, £2 plus 'the bed ... whereon my Servants do usually lodge'. Robert's wife Sarah, too, was left just £1, but their infant son John the future Slaymaker received a more valuable item, 'my two Iron Kittles'. Robert died 1716, intestate, but from Sarah's will, made ten years later, there is more to be learnt. To her son John she left 'all the stock belonging to the Slaymaking trade left by my late husband Robert, with my Shopp Book and my furnace standing in my Brew house'. By this time the son John had married and was, I am sure, living at Scarth. Sarah's will tells a little more. Her other three children, James, Robert and Sarah were to inherit jointly 'my dwelling house in Newtown'. It reads as if this Wilshere family had lived there, but in Sarah's later years her Newtown house had been leased out to three tenants, so by that time the Wilsheres had moved away.

The oldest Poor Rate book for Winsley covers much of this period.[4] It is a magnificent big, thick, leather bound tome covering some forty years from 1702, and in it we find Robert Wilshere starting in 1708 to pay the 1d. (nominal) rate on his house, his contribution for the relief of the poor. Is this the year he acquired that Newtown house? Or had he bought it some time before, but the rating authorities only woke up to the purchase in that year? Similarly, the rate book shows that John Wilshere the Slaymaker began to pay the annual Poor Rate on a 1d house, evidently on Scarth, in 1721. Again we ask who had it in the previous thirty years, if indeed it was the old Wilshere's house. All in all, we can only assume the evidence is strong enough – that Scarth probably was the old family house, but the verdict must remain not proven.

One further problem remains – why is it called Scarth? The previous name, Rock House, was used until 1925, and soon after the house was purchased by Captain W. R. C.Moorsom, and the link is with the Moorsoms and Scarths, two of the 'Bay families' at Robin Hood's Bay near Whitby on the north Yorkshire coast. In the 18th century a number of these families bought or shared boats in which they carried coal, and the like cargoes far and wide to the Baltic ports and the Mediterranean out from Whitby's good harbour. Richard Moorsom, in partnership with Thomas Scarth also prospered in whale fishing. Eventually they owned eight ships. Richard's son Robert, who married Eleanor Scarth, joined the Navy. He had a very distinguished Naval career, and was Captain of the Revenge at the battle of Trafalgar. His descendant, Captain Moorsom, when he bought the house at Winsley, was anxious to commemorate the name of his ancestor's highly esteemed partner, and therefore gave the name Scarth to his own house.[5]

The name Scarth was not, however, unknown in Turleigh quite independently before this time. From the 'Turleigh 2000' book we learn that Major Leverson Scarth who retired from the army in 1911, purchased property in Turleigh including Uplands House and Brooklands, which is now Turleigh House. He was born in Bath in 1851, but his family came from Staindrop in County Durham. Major Scarth moved away after his wife's death in 1919 but returned soon after to live at Turleigh Lodge (now Turleigh Cottage) where he died in 1925. He is remembered for founding the Turleigh Village Club to the great benefit of all those dwelling there for very many years.

Before continuing the life of John Wilshire, a few words about John's younger brother James Wilshire will fill out the story. A weaver like his brother, James also was active in village affairs, and in 1728 he married Ann Dagger, of the old Winsley family. There were three sons and four daughters of the marriage, all the men folk being weavers. In 1748 James Wilshere

The lion on the front of No.146 may have been the work of an apprentice of a Winsley stonemason's firm.

The gateway with an arch at no.146.

commenced to pay the poor rate for a house in the village, which remained in his family until 1811. The house deeds[6] make it clear that this was no. 146, later sometimes known as Lambourne House. It stands on the north side of the village lane, west of the church, facing the Pound, with a lion's head on the upper floor. There are a number of features that help to date the oldest part to about 1720 or soon after. The sitting room has a large stack with a wide fire-arch of the style of the early years of the 18th century and the ogee moulded mullions of the casement windows tell the same story. The weaving shop was evidently the western room of this older part of the house. For one thing, its windows, front and back, are noticeably wider than those of the rest of the house, giving the extra light the work needed.

Low down in the end wall, too, are two curiously shaped alcoves, about 3 foot high, with their sills only about 9 inches above the floor[7], and each with a small recess for a lighted candle in the wall above it. One guesses they were for something to do with weaving, but what? Their purpose may be similar to what a friend says she has seen in Nepal. Apparently somewhat similar low alcoves are to be found in weavers houses in that country. The weavers sit in them at their work, facing their looms. Another feature of the room is more often seen. At some time in the past the floorboards of the room above must have become rotten, but instead of replacing them, a second layer of boards was laid on top of the first, with the boards at right angles to the old ones[8]. Inevitably, these too became infected by the trouble and the whole have had to be replaced.

Was this alcove, one of two in No 146, something to do with weaving?

James died in 1752, at the height of a smallpox epidemic, and he may have been a victim. His house probably descended to his sons, first to James junior, his eldest, and later to John, described as a weaver and shopkeeper; and there are features in the house recalling this activity. It may have been about then that the initials 'M. W' were scratched on a window pane, perhaps by Mary, the daughter of the James senior.

Strangely, James Wilshire's daughter Ann was the only one of his children to marry. Was this, perhaps, a family living under strict parental discipline? The reason cannot have been that all available hands were needed to make ends meet, for the family were reasonably well off. Ann's husband was a thatcher, William Godwin. When their only child, a daughter Ann, grew up, she was for many years housekeeper for her three old surviving bachelor uncles, the last of whom, John, was 79 years old when he died in 1819. Ann had only married the year before, when both the house and three cottages, Nos. 135 to 137 next to the Wheatsheaf were settled on her, together with a dowry of £40. Her bridegroom Joseph Smallcombe had been born and grew up at Parsonage Farm and was by this time farming the parsonage land belonging to Church Farm (confusingly known at the time as Winsley Farm). Sadly, this was a short lived marriage, for Ann died in 1823. It was probably during these years that the Regency style eastern extension was added to the house, for the rating of the house jumped up from 1d to 1½d in about 1816, the size of increase one would expect for such an extension to the house.

Returning now to the senior branch of the family, John Wilshire was nicknamed 'Slaymaker' to distinguish him from other John Wiltshires in Winsley – John Wiltshire of Turlyn (Turleigh), John of Westwood, and a second John of Winsley. A slaymaker means a loom maker, for a slay was a vital moving part of a loom, beating the successive threads of the weft of the cloth firmly together. The Slaymaker evidently used to lease out his looms to neighbouring weavers working in their own homes, and in his will he bequeathed looms to four of these men.

John, as we saw, was following his father's trade. His brothers were both weavers. He himself was born before 1686, for in that year he was mentioned in his grandfather's will – 'to John my grandchild the lease of my two great kettles'. In 1716 John was married at Winsley to Priscilla Morris, a daughter of the Turleigh blacksmith. There had already been earlier marriage connections between the two families, for her grandmother Priscilla Wilshire had married an earlier Peter Morris.

The slaymaker took an active part in village affairs – as juryman, as churchwarden, and serving for many years on the parish vestry which, among other things, decided the year's poor rate. And he defended the villagers when they were accused by the Bradford authorities of neglecting to repair the road up through Turley. This was at about the time, July 1731, when the new bridge over the River Avon had just been built at the bottom of Winsley Hill. The local roads were evidently suffering from the resulting increase of traffic. Another side of Wilsher's character, his support for Methodism, will have arisen from John Wesley's visit to the village in 1739.

In subsequent years Wilshire acquired various properties – in 1733, for instance, a 3½d. house in Cottles Lane at Turleigh. It is now two houses, Innox and Stoneleigh, separated by a gap where a small in-fill building has been pulled down. This he bought from one Lewis, who perhaps gave his name to Lewis's Hill, up behind these houses. The next year Wilshere's rates went up by a further 4d because he had acquired 4 acres of woodland at Oaky Coppice from James Miles. This we can locate, for Wilshire's Barn can still be seen across a large field, no longer a coppice, on the south side of the main Bradford road midway between the tops of Cottles Lane and Wine Street. And in 1741 a deed[9] reveals that he bought some parsonage land at Turleigh which came on the market when the clothier Anthony Druce went bankrupt in the course of building Druce's Hill House in Bradford.

John Wilshire died on the 28th November 1757. He was found dead in the road from Bradford to Bath, apparently from natural causes[10]. The house he lived in and the adjoining Longhaises Garden he left of course to Priscilla his wife, with the reversion of the freehold to William, his youngest son. Priscilla also kept her husband's seat in Winsley Church between the Chancel and Abel Broad's seat. His eldest son Robert inherited the bakery at Turleigh, and his daughters Priscilla and Elizabeth the two cottages in Cottles Lane. After the death of John Wilshire's son William in 1785, Scarth was left to his widow Sarah, and after her death in 1805, jointly to their eight surviving sons and daughters.[11] Then, as we saw, when a couple of years later the Methodist group in the village decided to build their earliest chapel here, including a caretaker's cottage, it was the Wilshires who leased them a suitable plot of land in their garden at Scarth at a peppercorn rent. Scarth itself was then actually in the hands of William Wilshere's son in law John Gould and his wife Ann. Gould was later a coal merchant at Combe Down, and in the 1970s I remember Gould's firm still delivered coal in Winsley. Scarth was sold in 1835 to William Duck the village carpenter, a very skilful craftsman. The TA map shows that by 1841 the chapel and cottage buildings had been extended eastwards probably as a row of cottages, which in the 1887 O.S. map had disappeared again. The Tithe Map shows too that at that time there was a timber yard on the corner plot where the Social Club now is. W.W. Wheatley's painting looking across to this from the Seven Stars about this time shows an attractive cottage standing there, with another behind the village well – the one now beneath the bus shelter. Hidden behind these was a group of other cottages, then empty. The artist has

W.W.Wheatley painting, c. 1850. Road outside the Seven Stars. These cottages were burnt down in the 1863 fire. The well is now covered by the bus shelter. Church Cottages are on the right.

moved the church tower into a prominent position in the picture – it should really have been hidden behind the cottages. The year, 1841 also saw the first detailed national Census, and it confirms that William Duck and his 20 year old son Thomas lived at Scarth, running the carpentry business. William died about 1860, and in 1863 disaster hit the family, in the shape of the Great Fire of Winsley[12]. The timber yard and cottages were destroyed, but fortunately Scarth was not harmed.

On the south side of the village lane, near the corner where the Drung joins it, a small house has over the last centuries gradually grown into a long building, now made up of three individual homes, numbered 126 to 128. Till fairly recently there used to be a statue of Nelson (or was it Napoleon?) and a font, perhaps from the old parish church, in the front garden of the smaller central house, no. 127, a reminder of the time when these were the homes of a quarrying and stoneworking family. The house seems likely to have started sometime around 1700 as just a single house, now divided into the two northern houses 126 and 127, to which the tall southernmost house, no 128, was not added until the early nineteenth century. The two southern houses, which are now in the same ownership, were recorded recently by the Wiltshire Buildings Record. This report concludes that 'No. 127 was probably on a single room plan from the early 18th century... It was extended, re-faced and altered in the early to

The cottages of the Broad family's farm in the 18th century. (Nos.126, 127 and 128)

mid 19th century. It retained the older roof trusses and has an attic entrance (leading through) into no.126 adjoining. No 128 has a datestone of 1814 on its three storey ashlar front.' We have already mentioned 12th century sherds being found in the back garden of this house. The north house (126), being in a separate ownership, was not recorded with the others, but its ground floor had previously been examined by the authors.[13] It appears to have developed in a similar way to no. 127. However, whereas the latter has pairs of bordered sash windows at the front on each floor, no.126 has three light casements, so it looks as if its re-facing may have occurred rather earlier than 127's. It has a mansard roof, usually a late 18th or early 19th century feature. Inside, a couple of 17th century chamfered axial beams span the ground floor rooms. A large cellar with bread and brewing ovens is under the north room. It was later extended out under the road with a stone vault, and has so far managed to support the modern day traffic.

Since writing these pages, a relic of an older wall has been identified, projecting into the back garden of no. 127. It is appreciably thicker (28 in., or more if plastered, as against 24 in. of the latter) and could be a century older.

Ignoring 'the Cottage and Garden adjoining at the rear thereof (i.e. of no 128) in the occupation of William Tucker' as described in the 1879 sale particulars,[14] and shown in the Tithe map, as well as the many outhouses that came and went behind the two older houses, there are some features that

No.128, Ivy Cottage, built by Ambrose Heal in 1814, led to his going bankrupt.

make one wonder if those two may in fact have started life as a single house. A thick stone wall runs along the back of the two of them, and they have a thinner ashlar front wall, which probably replaced an earlier timber framed common front during their 19th century re-facing. After all, Cornelius Broad from Box, the likely builder, and several of his sons are often described as carpenters as well as masons. The south end wall of 127 is of similar thickness to the rear one, and it seems probable that the north wall of 126 was also the same before the digging of the cellar led to its replacement. So the pre-refacing plan of these two houses, with the very wide chimney stack between no.126 with its two rooms and no 127 with only one, suggests they started as a single house with a typical seventeenth century three-roomed plan. Its front door would have led into a lobby in front of the chimney stack – in fact a typical 'lobby entrance house' of the second half of the 17th or early 18th century.[15] That theory would explain the unusual thickness of the stack. When the old front wall was taken down for the refacing, the two houses were given their separate new front doors, and all trace of the old lobby doorway doubtless disappeared. In the attic however, we still have the wee door behind the stack connecting the two halves, another sign of a typical 17th century plan. And attached to the back of no 127 there is what may well have been a dairy, again typical of the period. An unexplained feature is that the fronts of the two houses are at a slight angle to each other. It does not seem possible to see whether there are similar changes of line in the rear walls or the ridges of the roofs.[16]

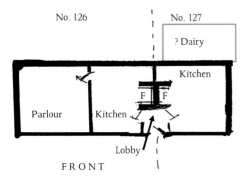

A lobby entry house around 1700: perhaps the Broad house (nos. 126 and 127) began like this.

A major event in the story of the growth of these houses must have been the building of no. 128, the new south house in 1814. The builder, Ambrose Heal, was a stonemason who lived at the other end of the row, and Thomas Smith was in between at no. 127. The Poor Rate book shows that the two men had been tenants of Heal's father in law, James Dagger, but Heal had bought the whole row outright a couple of years before. From here we can follow their story back in the rate books,[4] with only a few wobbles to its beginning in 1702, the earliest surviving book. In that year Cornelius Broad paid the rate on a 1d house – which was it, 126 or 127? There probably were earlier payments, but if so those records are lost. The Broads had come from Box to Turleigh where the family built Uplands. Later, leaving that house as the family home, Cornelius may have moved up to Winsley, where he was living in 1702. Unfortunately he died the next year, so the trail is lost immediately. We can only pick it up again in 1708 when 'Widdo Brode' took up the payments. Her rate was raised to 2d from 1712 – no reason is given. The house passed from Cornelius to his son John (died 1728) and then his grandson the younger John who married Mary, a sister of John Wilshere the slaymaker. The 2d rate continued to be paid by John Broad until 1782. Then these payments ceased.

The rate books show that the Broads also had a second house in Winsley – a 1½d house, acquired or perhaps built by Abel Broad in 1734 Again, they give no idea who had the house before him, or which house it was. There were plenty of Abel Broads in Winsley in the 18th century, but the only one around in 1734 was Cornelius's youngest son, born about 1694. He grew up in Turleigh, a carpenter and mason, but, somewhere around 1720, moved to Doulting near Shepton Mallet to work in the famous stone quarries there. He married a Doulting girl, Mary Rossiter, and brought her back to Winsley about 1734. His son Abel junior was born that year and maybe the move was prompted by the fact that no. 126 had just become vacant. 1734 was an eventful year for the whole Broad family and may have put quite a strain on their resources, for it was the year when the four brothers bought Burghope back from their Bath cousins.

The 1½d rating of Abel's house went up to 2d in 1738 and to 2½ d in 1779. Then in 1782, the payments for Cornelius' house ceased, and evidently Abel's grandson (another Abel, of course) acquired that house too. The Poor Rate assessors eventually waked up to the purchase, and in 1789 they put Abel's rating up by another 1d. It seems to confirm that Cornelius's house in 1702 was indeed no.127. Various reasons may lie behind the earlier rate rises – new building, say, or a new rate being charged on young Abel's alehouse business. A brewer and baker, he had his ovens and furnaces in his cellar at no.126, with the alehouse above. The cellar extension would have made a cool store for his stock. But we are in Abel trouble here – which Broad family did the Abel of the 1780s belong to? He died young in 1786, so it was his widow Mary who was

The three Broad cherubim on Abel's tombstone

paying the later rates. There is a bit of village scandal involved here. Abel's tombstone in the churchyard, once easy to read, but now practically illegible, bore the three charming infant faces of his daughters Mary, Elinor and Sarah. The children were all given the name of Butler Broad for they were born before Abel Broad married their mother Mary Butler – if he ever did.

The houses remained in Abel Broad's name until 1808, and then for several years they were owned by James Dagger who had married Broad's daughter Mary Butler Broad. According to the TA schedule of 1841, there was a field called 'Late Dagger's' at the top of the tramway that runs down from the Murhill quarry to its wharf on the canal below. So by that date James had sold some land to James Baber, the quarry owner at Murhill House. In 1809 the building of the canal was just complete, and Dagger, who also had much of the land the tramway was built on, must have done well out of the sale.

It was not till the end of the 18th century that it was decided to build the central section of the canal. The two ends, from the Thames up the Kennet to Newbury and from Bristol up the Avon to Bath were already prosperous, but there does not seem to have been much local enthusiasm for joining the two ends. The route finally chosen for the middle section is more or less on the line of John Rennie's survey in 1793, but half of the Winsley section of this does not follow the line he suggested. Instead of crossing the Avon below Conkwell at Dundas, the canal was to have stayed on the Somerset bank of the river till just upstream of the Stokesford bridge at the foot of Winsley Hill[17] and then crossed the river to rejoin the present route. The Winsley section of the canal was always troublesome and was long known as the Dry Section that was always leaking.

James Dagger had tenants at the two Broad houses, Ambrose Heal probably at no.126 and Thomas Smith at no.127. Heal, a stone mason, was I imagine, the builder of a number of cottages which Dagger put up on his land at the side of the quarry tramway. It must have been a time of growing prosperity for stone quarries, with the new canal transport to take the stone easily to London and Bristol, in contrast to the problems for the spinning and weaving in the cottages as many of the cloth mills closed. .

Another Ambrose Heal, a cousin, went to London about this time, where he founded the well known furniture store in Tottenham Court Road. He was followed by several generations of Ambrose Heals who were eminent furniture designers for the firm. His namesake at Winsley, on the other hand, was an active house builder. At some time between 1814 and 1817, he bought both 126 and 127[18], and, as the 1814 datestone shows, built no.128 on the south end of the row for himself. The cottages 147 to 149 in Conkwell Lane opposite the church were also his work. His son John Lea Heal, who for a time was Joseph Smallcombe's tenant in part of no.146, worked with his father on the regency style extension of that house perhaps about 1818 and himself built Bleak House in similar style soon after. In the 20th century this house was long occupied by

Bleak House, built by John Heal in 1824 – the date is on the parapet.

Mr Harbutt, the inventor and manufacturer of Plasticine. Ambrose seems to have overstretched himself in all this, and ran into difficulties in financing his work; by 1820 he had to raise a £500 mortgage on his own house from Thomas Lavington, a Westbury farmer. A letter from Thomas Hosier Saunders, a Bradford clothier and J.P. tells what happened next.[19] Writing to a solicitor acting for Lavington, Saunders writes:

Dear Sir,
One of the Overseers Mr.Ambrose Heal has lately absconded having collected about 200 or 250 pounds of the poor rates and is unable to pay it to me as parish treasurer without raising it either by sale or second mortgage on his house and Land at Winsley already in mortgage to your client Farmer Thomas Lavington for a sum, altogether I understand including principal Interest and other debts due to Mr Lavington, of

about £520. I am in possession of all Heal's Goods &c. under a Magistrate's Warrant of Distress issued in virtue of our local Act, but as it appears Heal has about sufficient to pay all his debts. I do not want to force a sale and ruin the Man, particularly as I can get the money raised through Mr. Luxford (a Bradford solicitor) on a second mortgage of the property included in your client's.

Will you therefore send Mr Luxford down by the Monday Morning Mail a Letter with a short abstract of Mr Lavington's Mortgage deeds stating the full parish and such other particulars as will enable him to get the second mortgage ready so as to remove the distress and allow Heal to return home and sell the house and in conjunction with the Mortgages to pay off all that will be due. As Treasurer for the parish I cannot wait for a sale of the house and if this plan of second mortgage be not accepted Heal must go to prison on the parish account until the money could be raised by sale as the goods alone are not sufficient.

Meanwhile Heal's goods were distrained by George Butt, the Winsley Tithingman ' (i.e. constable), a neighbour of Heal's. An inventory[20] taken by order of the J.P.s will be found in the notes. Valued at £182. 2s. 9d., they make interesting reading. Besides the household goods, there was stone and ashlar at the Murhill quarry, and more of it at the wharf and one boat on the 'Cannall'.

Then, although the second mortgage had been agreed and its preparation was well in hand, it was obviously feared Heal's property would be sold off before the money matters could be completed – Ann Heal particularly was very worried that some obstacle would lead to her belongings being sold off as well as her husband's and she wrote to Saunders a couple of times over the next fortnight to ask that the sale be delayed for a week. Then on the 30th September Saunders notes 'George Butt discharged from possession on Ambrose Heal signing second Mortgage to Mr. Luxford ...' The remaining ends were very soon tied up satisfactorily and the Heals were able to resume their occupation of no. 128 for the rest of his life, and followed after his death by his son John Lea Heal.

In the absence of deeds for the property at that time, a later sale required John Lea Heal and his wife Elizabeth jointly to make a solemn declaration[21] to confirm the legality of the changes of ownership. It reads that after a few years Edward Luxford, the mortgagee, foreclosed and the cottages and houses became his property, and so it remained in his family until, in October 1840, a niece of Luxford's sold it to Richard King. To fix the date when King bought it, Elizabeth added her own declaration: 'I distinctly remember the purchase of the said property by the said King and that I also distinctly remember the then wife of the said Richard King coming to my house subsequently to the purchase and inspecting the property and entering into conversation with me as to the purchase by her husband. These facts are particularly impressed upon my memory by the fact that the time they occurred was 2 or 3 months previously to the birth of my eldest son who was born on the 30th day of October 1840.'

Richard King died in 1870 and in 1879 his very extensive Winsley property was to be sold at auction at the Swan Hotel in Bradford[22]. His three houses, numbers 126 to 128, are described in the sale particulars in: Lot 23 (No.128) was 'a Substantially built Freehold Dwelling House in the centre of Winsley in the occupation of Mrs. King, now age 75', and Lot 24, the other houses, 'Two Freehold Dwelling houses and premises occupied by Mrs. Ward and Mr. Forster, and the newly erected Stable and Coach House with the Granary over it.

Epilogue

T HE HISTORY of Winsley now approaches its rather arbitrarily chosen mid point, the Tithe Apportionment year of 1841 that separates the early years from those that lead on up to the present. These years around 1841 were ones in which, more rapidly than in earlier times, old ways and features were being replaced by new ones leading towards a more modern world. In that very year one such change was the completion, with the opening of the Box tunnel, of the final section of that novelty, Brunel's Great Western Railway to London and the inauguration of the through train service. Local consequences soon followed. In that autumn the *Devizes and Wiltshire Gazette* carried an advertisement of Stephen Mizen's new 'Bradford Omnibus'. This coach was to leave the Lamb Inn next to Bradford town bridge at half past seven daily, to catch the 10 a.m. train at Chippenham. It would return from Chippenham on the arrival of the 4 p.m. train and reach Bradford in time for the Trowbridge omnibus.[23]

Similarly the old system of poor relief had recently been brought up to date. Under the old system, Poor Rates, levied on sufficiently prosperous citizens since Elizabethan times, were distributed to those in need by voluntary Overseers in each parish. This system had become unworkable and was abolished in 1833, after many unsuccessful attempts to cure its faults. Instead, parishes were now to be grouped into larger Poor Law Unions, setting up the system of Union Workhouses.[24] This was not the earliest poor house in Bradford. The parish's Vestry minutes for 1725 record a much earlier agreement made with Thomas Methuen for setting one up. It proposed that 'Tenements and garden called the Dutch Barton or Coombs, now in the occupation of Eliz. Orpen widow...and others , together with the way leading from Church Street to the tenements' be used ' ....to hold to the Trustees for managing ye Work house... the same to be repaired and built at the Charge of the Parish and kept in repair by the parish, with Methuen to pay the taxes'.[25]

One always imagines that the size of a village and its population varied little and slowly in former days, but at first sight that seems not to be the story told by the census returns. Once again, 1841 was a dividing year, when the first detailed Census was taken, recording the names of all the village's inhabitants. There had been regular ten yearly censuses since the beginning of the century but they only gave the total numbers for each tithing, but without their names. Quoting from the V.C.H., the old tithing had 2316 inhabitants in 1811, rising to 3000 in 1821 and 1831 while the cloth industry was still flourishing after the end of the Napoleonic wars. But ten years later the majority of Bradford clothing mills were closing and our population dropped to 2267 in 1841 and only 1587 in 1851. The place must have looked empty. A guess would be that these fluctuations were mainly in the upper, Bradford part of Winsley, while the numbers in and around the village itself and its hamlets stayed fairly steady, perhaps at about six hundred or so. According to the later censuses the village population seems indeed to have continued at about that six hundred mark for the rest of the century[26] .

The rebuilding of Winsley church in the mid 19th century is one of several such works initiated by the Rev. Henry Harvey, the vicar of Bradford, the parish Winsley still belonged to at that time. Related to William Cowper, and descended on his mother's side from John Donne, Harvey came to Bradford in 1835 (though apparently appointed some years before). His parish still included Winsley at that date. These were the years of the greatest hardship which saw the near destruction of the town's cloth industry. At a meeting at Devizes[27] in 1841 he spoke of his feelings at the distress of Bradford's work people in that cold winter. 'Let anyone witness and observe, as I have done, week after week, the increasing suffering of our poor, and with it, as at the present time has been the case, their admirable patience and good conduct... meet them daily carrying their little property for disposal, or shifting from a commodious dwelling to one of smaller dimensions or less convenience ... notice their dejected and emaciated appearance ... hear continuously their tales of want, told for the most part with simplicity, and though but little able to supply them with the most scant relief, never experiencing a single act or word of rudeness or incivility...' It was no doubt the strength of these feelings that led him to be a moving spirit in the programme of relief work – particularly building work – in the parish. Besides several schools, Harvey is remembered for the initial building of Christ Church at the top of Mason's Lane, and the rebuilding of village churches, first at Atworth, soon after he arrived here and later, at Winsley in 1839. Others of his churches received partial reconstruction and extensive repairs in a typical Victorian way.

Here at Winsley, after much discussion, a proclamation from the Bishop of Salisbury to the Vicar, dated the 18th March 1840 reads that 'Whereas it hath been represented to us by the Vicar Churchwarden and other Inhabitants of the Chapelry of Winsley that the Chapel ... is in a dilapidated state and too small to afford suitable accommodation to the inhabitants of the said Chapelry ... , of whom 600 reside near the chapel, and the Chapel having accommodation for 230 persons only, That at a Vestry held in the Chapel on December 12th 1839 it was ... resolved to take down the said Chapel, except the Tower, and build a substantial, convenient

The Barn, probably much of it built of stone from the old parish church.

and durable Chapel on a larger scale' connected with the present Tower ...' to accommodate 412 persons and reusing as much as possible of the old masonry...'. The estimated expense was £735, and voluntary contributions, above all from Ann Attwood of Turleigh Manor, and a number of large grants had already raised most of this. The proclamation was to be kept in the Diocesan Archives at Salisbury[28]. And of course a copy was to be published by fixing it on the Outer Door of the chapel. Two years later the work was finished. Looking at Buckler's picture of the old church, one may regret its loss, but it seems to have become much too small. But was it really in such a dilapidated state?

The old church seems to have housed many of the memorials of village worthies of earlier days. Its nave and chancel were aligned on the east of the tower in the normal way. The reason for building the new church parallel to the old one on its north side was so as to be able to continue to use the old one for worship until its successor was ready to move into. According to Pevsner[29], who called the interior uninspired, it was built to plans by R.S. Pope of Bristol. And much of the old stonework was reused in The Barn and, one imagines, in many other houses nearby as well as the new church itself.

Fortunately the church was not affected by the disastrous fire that occurred twenty years later, in 1863, at Thomas Duck's woodyard on the other side of the lane. That story is told in the paper the following Saturday.

ALARMING FIRE AT WINSLEY

On Tuesday afternoon a fire occurred in the village, and at one time threatened the most serious consequences; as it was, it has left ample evidence of its ravages. It seems that close to the Seven Stars Inn stood some cottages, which fortunately were unoccupied. Some children were playing beneath one of the doorways at the back, and made a bonfire with some loose straws. The wind blowing violently at the time, the fire communicated with the thatched roof of one of the cottages and soon the whole was in flames. The children, alarmed at the results of their imprudence,

raised an alarm, and a number of villagers were quickly on the spot. On account of the dryness of the thatch and the scarcity of water, all efforts to subdue the fire were fruitless, and the village could do little else than watch the progress of the devouring element. Aided by the high wind which was blowing, the flames soon wrapped the three cottages in a mass of fire and reduced them to ruins. The fire next seized on a stable and hayrick adjoining, which it also destroyed. Large flakes of fire were whirled into the timber yard occupied conjointly by Messrs. Duck and Broad, and serious apprehensions were entertained for the safety of the timber, but it was removed and all danger in that quarter averted. Not so, however with regard to a carthouse and straw barton, in connection with the farm occupied by Mrs. Pinchin, which were destroyed. Attention was then moved to the Seven Stars Inn, the thatched roof of which had ignited in several places, from the flakes of fire being carried into the thatch by the wind. Several men got upon the roof, and as fast as water could be procured, kept pouring it upon the burning portions of the roof, and it was only by persevering in this manner that the building was saved. Soon after the fire was discovered Inspector Pitney of Bradford was on the spot, and with the assistance of P.C.s Millard, Mathers and Taylor and a large number of men and even of women and children, exerted themselves to the utmost to prevent the spread of the fire, which was no easy task, considering the only supply of water nearer than Turley was the well at Winsley. Notwithstanding this difficulty all worked well, and but for the prompt assistance rendered by the police, it was just possible that a considerable portion of the village could have been laid in ruins. The cottages were the property of Mr John Sheppard of Bradford and the stable and hayrick were the property of messrs T & C Taylor of Winsley. The losses are, we believe, covered by insurance.... Application was made for the use of one of the Bradford fire engines, but the Town Commissioners, we are informed, declined to grant the request, unless a guarantee could be given that a man should be put in charge of it and see that it was safely returned.
[From the *Trowbridge and N. Wilts Advertiser*, Saturday 2nd May, 1863]

It is commonly believed that the fire destroyed the old parish church. This cannot be true, for the new church had been built more than twenty years before the fire. It is easy to see how the story arose, for the fire was, however, not a total disaster. Ten years after it, when a site was needed for the new Winsley Church School – not the new church – where better could it be built! And there the school stood for the next hundred years till, in 1973, with the coming of its successor, the 'Old School' has become the Social Club.

And so we bring our Odds to an End!

virtue of his office, and would have to pass on to his successor at the end of his term of office.

26. Ann Williams, in 'The Knights of Shaftesbury Abbey', *Anglo-Norman Studies* viii, 1985, discusses the carriage service and the duties of the Riding Men. See also her important paper 'The Abbey Tenants and Servants in the 12th Century' in *Studies in the Early History of Shaftesbury Abbey*, ed L. Keen.

27. Is this perhaps the standard medieval abbreviation: maria may be the abbreviation for maneria = manors?

Chapter 3

1. *Crown pleas of the Wiltshire eyre, 1249*, Ed. C.A.F. Meekings, W(iltshire) R(ecord) S(ociety), Vol. XVI, 1961. 'Civil pleas of the Wiltshire eyre, 1249', Ed, M. T. Clanchy, W.R.S. Vol; XXVI, 1971.

2. 'Deodand: an object which contributed to the death of someone ... was believed to share the guilt of his death. The object or its worth was forfeit to the crown, who applied it for charitable purposes.' [The Local Historian's Encyclopedia']

3. Shaftesbury Cartulary ut supra, fo. 33

4. Reg. Wyvil, ref. D1/2/3 at W.R.O. There is an eighteenth century translation at the Bristol Record office, ref DC/E/27/1.

5. A good explanation of impropriation is in C. G. Coulton, *Medieval Panorama*, C.U.P., 1949. For some details of the impropriation of the Bradford church, see *V.C.H. Wilts.* vol VII, p.24. Royal licence to appropriate, 1332, [Cal Pat. 1330 – 4, 364]. Consent of the Pope was obtained 1343, [Cal. Papal Reg. iii, 137].

6. *Tax Eccl.* (Record Commission, 1806)= *Taxatio Nicholas I, 1291*, at W.R.O..

7. Great tithes were levied on corn, hay and wood by the rector; small tithes from all other sources went to the resident vicar.

8. Buckler's water colour drawings at the library of W.A.N.H.S., Devizes. W. W. Wheatley also made several paintings of the church just before it was demolished.

9. See 'Medieval Agriculture' in *V.C.H., Wilts.* vol IV

10. Lay Subsidy,'Fifteenths and Tenths', 1 Ed III, ref E 179/196/7 at P.R.O.

11. Lay Subsidy,'Fifteenths and Tenths', 7 Ed III, ref E 179/196/8 at P.R.O. The latter is printed in *The Wiltshire Tax List of 1332*, Wilts. Rec. Soc. vol. 45 (1989).

12. E179/196/52, 1 Ric.II, 1378 at P.R.O.

13. In the Bradford Poll Tax roll (ref 11) the entry is 'Simon Corsoule (of Corsley?) clericus'. In this context clericus will not mean clergyman, for the clergy were assessed under a different system from the laity's poll tax. Latham, *Revised Medieval Latin Word-List* gives numerous possible lay clerks called clericus – a town or market clerk is perhaps the most likely.

14. Accounts of Bradford Manor, 1367 to 1392. ref 1742/6786 at W.R.O. Transcription of the account for year 15 Joan Formage, 1376, deposited at W.R.O.

15. A roll of the accounts of Wraxall tithing for the same years existed till recently but has been missing since before these Methuen archives were deposited at the W.R.O. It suggests that a similar roll for Winsley may once have existed.

16. This would have been the state of affairs at least since the impropriation of 1349.

17. Maurice Beresford,*History on the Ground*, Methuen,1971, pp69,70.

18. W.R.O. 1742/6786: account for year 15 of Joan Formage, Firma terrarum nos. 7, 9, 11, 15, 16, 17.

19. Ib. Exitus Operum, no. 5,

20. Until the 19th century this was still being paid as 'larding money'.

21. *Abstracts of Feet of Fines Edward III*, Ed. C. R. Elrington, Wilts. Rec.Soc, vol xxix (1974), no. 490.

22. W.R.O. 1752/6786 again, entry under 'Cachepolwyke'. It reads: 18d. de locag. 1 scabell quondam Thome Pylk stant ex opposito tenemente Ricardi Gibbes dimiss. Johi. Marys et Willmo. atte Clyve ad term vite pac° ad 4 termini.

23. *The Edington Carulary*, Ed. Janet H. Stevenson, Wilts. Re.Soc. vol 42, 1987.

24. Both men had the same half virgate and had to reap half an acre of the harvest. Walter also had to send one man for the haymaking at Yeamead and Muchelmead as well as a day's work in the vineyard.

25. W.R.O. 1742/3245 .

26. Court Book of Shaftesbury Abbey, 1488. W.R.O. ref 2667/12/48.

27. Court Book of the Abbess of Shaftesbury's estates, 1517-18, W.R.O. ref 1728/ 79.

28. A farundel was ¼ of a virgate, say about 7 acres.

29. Register of Bishop Edmond Awdley at W.R.O., ref. D1/2/14.

30. Though Winsley is not directly mentioned, it is worth noticing a fourth report in the bishop's register. One John Tropnell, a tiler of Bradford, who may have belonged to the Turleigh group, was condemned for relapsing into his former ways after abjuring them. It is difficult to see what his punishment was to be. Was there perhaps a link here with the Thomas Tropnell (or Traynell) who, according to reliable Bradford books, was burnt at the stake in 1532 in the market place at Bradford, for denying the same doctrine of transubstantiation.

31. Especially *Wiltshire Farmhouses and Cottages* and *Medieval Houses of Wiltshire*.

32. Report 17 of List 17. Tree ring dates from the Oxford Dendrochronology Laboratory. Dr Daniel Miles and others, published in *Vernacular Architecture*, vol. 37 (2006), p.122. The form of the truss and some small boards near its apex suggest a possible small louvre here.

33. Winsley Shield. Extract from letter of 21 Sept. 1983 from I.D.D.Eaves, Keeper of Armour at The Armouries, H.M.Tower of London, to the authors: 'This (shield) has indeed been lent to us (by the British Museum) and is now on show in the infantry case of our new Medieval Gallery in the White Tower. It bears our loan number AL 116/330. It is made of leather, reinforced on the outside with radiating strips and concentric rings of iron, bearing simple incised and punched decoration. In the centre is a hollow iron boss to accommodate the fist when gripping the iron reinforced wooden crossbar at the rear.

    Small, circular shields of this type, mainly used from the 'second' half of the 13th century to the first half of the 16th century, were known as 'bucklers'. They were normally carried by civilians, or unarmoured infantry, as a personal defence; typically in conjunction with a sword. Sword and buckler fighting constituted an early form of fencing: the buckler used to parry the opponent's sword. Some of the wilder characters among the fencers were referred to as 'swashbucklers' in the 16th century. Medieval bucklers are exceptionally scarce, and their dating is therefore difficult; particularly as contemporary illustrations suggest that their design changed little over the years. We have tentatively dated the Winsley buckler to the 15th century, but there is no real reason for excluding a date in the 14th century, or perhaps even in the early 16th century. The Winsley buckler is a very rare piece and comparison is virtually impossible'.

34. Benstede refs.are in Winterslow Inquisitions Post Mortem dated from 1274 to 1343, naming John de Benstede, 1324, his son and heir Edmund. In 1342 Winterslow Manor was held by Edward le Despenser of the heirs of Edward de Benstede, a minor. The last of the male line, Sir William de Benstede, died 1485. See D.N.B. article on John de Benstede.

Chapter 4.

1. This and most of these wills are at WRO.
2. J. H. Bettey, *The Suppression of the Monasteries in the West Country*, Alan Sutton, 1989.
3. Two Taxation Lists, 1545 and 1576, G.D. Ramsay, W.A.N.H.S., Records Branch, (now Wiltshire Record Society), Vol X, Devizes, 1954.
4. Bristol Record Office, Bristol Chapter estates, DC/E/27/2. See translation of the Winsley section below, Appendix 3.
5. Ib. DC/E/27/32 contains survey of Bradford prebend Manor in 1754, by Edward Burcombe. It refers to 'Two other Copyholds at Winsley held for 3 lives, called Guidings and Capons' with a later (1809?) pencil note: Wm Taylor (Blacksmith) & Jas.Eyles, 4 tenements' The Blacksmith's shop and cottages adjoining are Nos. 153-5.
6. A new Budbury Farm was built east of Budbury Place early in the 20th century. It is shown on the 1925 O.S. map.
7. WRO 1742/3245. and summary 212B/522
8. Westbury was prosperous enough to be assessed at £4 on goods for the 1576 Subsidy (ref. 3) and was a customary tenant in the 1570 rental ref. 12.
9. Twosting yron = toasting fork. A furnitude = a set of weapons/ armour for the militia. A jacke was a leather fighting jacket.
10. TA numbers 1178 &1311.
11. W.R.O. 217/6
12. British Library, Egertom Ms. 3653. I am grateful to Pam Slocombe for a copy of this document. The two William Druces must have been distinct persons, for they paid different rents.
13. W.R.O. ref. 1742/1999.
14. Ib. The TA shows a field called Hawcroft, No.1875, on the north side of the B3108 just east of the Cottles Lane crossroads, not a likely place for a stream but the land has been much disturbed. If this Hawcroft was much larger in the 16th century, it could perhaps have contained the source of a former stream running down Cottles Lane to Turley.
15. Will and inventory at W.R.O.
16. They were a barn, stall, waggon house and stable. All these have now gone, replaced by various buildings from the 19th century.
17. W.R.O. ref 947/1315.
18. W.R.O. 130/54a.
19. W.R.O. 947/1330.
20. Two indentures in possession of Mr & Mrs R.Silcox, leases to James Butter, 1688 & 1704.
21. They are described as 'de novo nuper edificat', newly, recently built. This could mean a new cottage on the site of a previous one or on a fresh site.
22. The TA map shows The Sands as a field north of the crossroads at Hartley. Was the old 'Sands' a general name for a large region north of the church, or were there two 'Sands' in 1600?
23. This court entry is of course in Latin with phrases headed Anglice, 'in English' in the original. I give a rough translation.
24. Alternatively, the deciding factor was perhaps that a subtenancy would mean a loss of rent? It is not stated whether the subtenant was occupying a separate house or a portion of the tenant's home.
25. The evidence from the ground floor is not so clear. The two cottages resemble a single 'hall

and crosswing' building, but the presence of the two closely spaced walls between the cottages probably make this unlikely.

26. 12 ft by 14 ft (375 by 420 cm). Surely Vennell's family must have occupied no. 140 as well as 141.
27. Nos. 143 & 144.
28. 'Cucking-stool (Dictionary): a chair to which disorderly women were tied and then ducked into water ... '

Chapter 5.

Many references in this chapter are to the W.R.O. 947/1315, which consists of two large bundles of manorial deeds, perhaps those passed over by the Kent family to Edward Thresher when he purchased the Manor around 1715. Suggested dating for the deeds here referred to are added in brackets, hoping to make their location possible.

1. P.D.A. Harvey, *Manorial Records*, British Records Association, 'Archives and the user', No.5, 1984.
2. Accounts of Bradford Manor, 1367 – 1392. W.R.O ref. 1742/6786.
3. P.D.A. Harvey, Ib p. 55.
4. Will; Arch Saum at W.R.O.
5. *V.C.H., Wilts*. vol VII. p.13. This grant of Bradford included appurtenances in Winsley. Bellingham, who died in 1549, was then Lord Deputy of Ireland.
6. W.R.O. ref. 947/1315.[e.g indenture dated 30 Nov. 12 James, 1615] 'Richard Bourke, Earl of Clanricard, president of the province of Connaght in the Realm of Ireland and one of the King's most honorable Privie Counsell in the Realm of Ireland.'
7. L.& P. Hen VIII , xvii, p.638.
8. Letter Patent C 66/ 1208, m. 2. Details in V.C.H. VOL VII p.13 – Elizabeth to Walsingham as C66/ 1148, for 1/40th of a knights fee. See also W.A.M.xli, p.218
9. Herald's Visitation of Wiltshire, 1599, p. . See also Isabel Ide, 'John Kent', W. A. M 88, p.91, (1995)
10. Wiltshire Heritage Museum Library, Devizes. See also I.Ide, Ib.p. 94.
11. Kent's work as Clerk of the Peace for the county is described in detail in the introduction to the Wiltshire Record Society's vol XI, *Wiltshire Quarter Sessions, 1736*, ed. G. D. Ramsay, (1954). .
12. *Abstracts of Wiltshire Inquisitions Post Mortem, Charles I*, W.A.N.H.S., Earl of Hertford, pp. 17 – 18, 20 – 31.
13. W.R.O. ref 130 / 54a. This is probably now called 'Turleigh Grange'.
14. 1 yardland = 1 virgate was most commonly reckoned to be a holding of about 30 acres, but very variable, say between 25 acres and 40 or more. The figure of 600 acres in the sale to Kent may be compared with the 633 acres of the manor at its sale in 1825 after the death of Mary Thresher. However numerous pieces of land had been bought and sold in the years between the two, so the comparison is not reliable.
15. The sale documents are in W.R.O. 947/1315. The main documents in the two instalments are dated 12 James (1614/15) and 13/15 James with additional deeds in 17 James and later. With the following abbreviations: -
M/T = messuage or tenement, YL = yardland, occ = in the tenure or occupation of T,W,H = in Turlinge, in Winnesley, in Haughe . m, pas, wd. = meadow, pasture, woodland . c. = called. cl. = close.

The holdings in the first sale were

1. M/T, 1YL, & certen Overlands, W, late occ. Richard Meade

2. M/T & 1 YL, T, occ Richard Meade

3. M/T & 1YL, W, late occ Richard Wilshere.

4. Cottage c. Lockscote, W, late occ. Alice & Richard Guydinge.

5. cl. pas Knoll Hill, W, 2 acres late Bartholomew Turgey exchanged with other land. These five now in occ John Kent thelder.

6. M/T, ½YL in T, M/T, ½YL in H, M/T ½YL ,W. all (?) sometymes Thos Brayes, then Thos Kippings, now Drew Druce.

7. M/T, two x ½YL, T & W, occ Drew Druce

8. M/T & 1 YL, T, occ Anthony Atkins.

9. M/T, ½ YL, T, occ John Wilshere.

10. M/T, 1YL & 1 Tofte of a Mess.& ½ YL sometymes Waches, W, occ John Hendy.

11. M/T, 1YL, W, occ Elizabeth Wilshere.

12. M/T,1YL, W, occ John Meade.

And all those several cottages & Gardens, W & T , occ Robert Wilkyns, Richard Atkyns, John Morrys, Henry Marshman, Edward Poole, Thomas Burche, James Warrs, Thomas Edmere, & Robert Wilshere.

And the second sale.

1. M & ½ hide & 1 YL (60 acres) land, m, wd, W, T, occ John Wythie.

2. M, 1YL, W, T, occ John Reynolds

3. M, 1YL, W, T, occ Edithe Reynoldes, widow.

4. M, 1 YL, W, T, occ Robert Huntlye

5. M & ½ YL, occ Bartholomewe Turgey & wife Doratheye.

6. M/Cottage, T, W, occ Edithe Bristowe widow.

16. Perhaps son of Edward Meade, c. 1570.

17. They were Robert Drewe of Southbroome, Christopher Potticarye, Lord of the manor of Stockton in the Wylie Valley, and John Stephens, who married Mary Kent. We have not found the relationship between Christopher Potticery and Jerome, whose daughter Anne married John Kent [II].

18. Lease to Willyam Allen in W.R.O. 947/ 1315. (c.1627)

19. P.c.c. Will at P.R.O. For the brass, see Edward Kite, (*The Monumental Brasses of Wiltshire*, 1860). pl. xxx.

20. Marriage settlement: 947/1315, (L & R dated 16/17 July 1674)

21. Elizabeth Kent lived with him at Weyhill after the death of her husband. He was perhaps her brother in law, for in his will, Thomas Kent calls him Uncle.

22. W. R. O. 947/1347 (c.1705).

23. Ib., several deeds c.1715, also 947/1347 and Indenture dated 7 Jan 1715 in 947/ 1315. There was no need for a royal 'Licence to Alienate' this time, as the manor was not being subdivided.

24. W, H, Jones, *Bradford -on -Avon*, annotation by John Beddoe, 1907, pp. 162-4.

25. For Chantry House; for Frankleigh Farm purchase, W.R.O. 217/4.

26. Bristol Record Office; ref. DG/E/27/45.

27. Booklets and indentures of land exchanges: W.R.O. ref 947/1334.

28. Ib. in Booklet 1.

29. K.H.Rogers, *Warp and Weft*, Barracuda Books Ltd, 1986, p.51.

30. W. R. O. ref 947/1334. .

31. Thresher tree in Jones, Bradford on Avon, p.129.

32. W. R. O. ref 947/931/1.
33. W. R. O. refs. 947 / 1714, various, also 816 / 16
34. Dyrham Park; see National Trust archive at the Gloucestershire Record Office.
35. W.R.O. ref 947 1349/ 1 & 2.contains much more detail,
36. W.R.O. ref. 947/ 1712
37. W.R.O. ref 947/1713.
38. Sale particulars, copy at W.R.O, and follow up letter in 947/1361 and 1362.
39. *Kelly's Directory, Wiltshire.*

Chapter 6

In old deeds, To Farm Letten means to lease, & a field of housing means a bay of a house. The
W.R.O. ref. 1742 contains the Methuen archives.

1. *Leland's Itinerary*, ed. Toulmin – Smith, i . 134
2. W.R.O. 1742 / 3265.
3. Catshill: – W. B. R. report on the Newtown brewery, Pam Slocombe.
4. W.R.O. 1742 / 4579 3244 & 3266. Others are 1742/4576, and 1742/4584. The Marchant
   petition is in W.R.O. 1742 / 3244
5. Note from Pam Slocombe: 'The Act of 1589 required that new cottages should have at least
   four acres of land attached, but this legislation was not enforced consistently'. In fact the
   Marchant petition shows how this requirement could be relaxed by the Quarter Sessions.
   The Spring 2004 issue of the Guardian Angel, (Bradford on Avon Preservation Trust)
   contains a note on William Audley, one of the Bradford petitioners.
6. W.R.O. 1742 / 4591., [21 March 3 Charles (1627)] deals with the quarry at Catshill. It reads:
   – Between (1) Elizabeth Blanchard of Budbury, widdowe, Robert Earle of Budbury, yeoman,
   and Elizabeth his wife, Michael Tidcombe of the Devizes, gent, and Susannah his wife and
   Joyce Blanchard the youngest daughter of the said Elizabeth Blanchard [Elizabeth Earle,
   Susannah Tidcombe and Joyce Blanchard were the three daughters of John and Elizabeth
   Blanchard] and (2) Thomas Bishopp of the towne and Countye of Southampton, yeoman
   Witnesseth that (1) in consideration of Fower pounds (paid to (2) and acknowledged) **Have**...
   to ffarme letten ... to (2) **All that Cotage** containing two feild of houseing adjoining to the
   north end of the cotage lyeing and being in the aforesaid hill called Catshill... now in the
   tenure or occupacion of one John Flowrence, Together with a lyttle plott of grownde
   extendinge from the Chymne of the said house...(to the). feelde of houseinge rounde the
   northe end of the said houseinge up to the Conyger there [Except and always reserved out
   of the demise and graunte unto (1) ..their heirs and assignes the stones and quarr of and
   for the diggyng in or upon the said litle plott of grownde with free ingresse and regresse to
   and for the sid (1) ... from tyme to tyme and at all tymes convenient to digg take and carry
   awaye the same stone without doeing annoyance or hert to the cottage aforsaid. And alsoe
   the said (1) for the consideracions aforesaid have likewise demised graunted and to farm
   letten .... to (2) one other litle garden plott or grownde lyeing in Cattshill ... between the
   Cottage nowe or hereto before in the tenure and occupacion of one Maude Burgis widow
   northward and the end of the cotage nowe or heretofore in the tenure of Jon Nicholls
   southward , **To Have or to hold &c.**
7. Report to Wilts.Bldgs Record by P.Slocombe.
8. W.R.O. 1742/3275 (John Earle of Budbury to Methuen), followed by various deeds, e.g.
   1742 / 3277, leases by Methuen, new cottage for sub tenants.

9. Turnpike Trust Acts 1774, 1817, ref. W.R.O. G13 / 990 /.,
10. ' ' ', 1819, W.R.O. G13/ 990/ 23.
11. On the Tithe Map, Says Green is TA1992[a], pasture; now part of Christ Church School.
12. Robert Haynes and Ivor Slocombe, *Wiltshire Toll Houses*, Hobnob Press, 2004.
13. From the late P.Beaven, Winsley.
14. *Abstracts of Wiltshire Inquisitiones Post Mortem, Charles I*; W.A.N.H.S., 1894, pp. 292, 421.
15. It has been suggested that these cottages may have been at Catshill or Tory.
16. Abstracts...,Ib. p.341. There seems to be some doubt if her name was Joyce or Joane.
17. *Accounts of the parliamentary garrisons of Great Chalfield and Malmesbury, 1645-6*, edited by J. H. P. Pafford (1940), Wiltshire Record Society. Vol II. By comparison, Wraxall provided 219 lb. and 1 chine of bacon, 1 barrel of beer, 9 lb of butter, 168 lb. of cheese, 20 loads of hay, 5 hens, 37 bushels of malt, besides oats and wheat.
18. Alan Dodge, *Freshford, the History of a Somerset Village*, Freshford Publications, 2000, p.64.
19. W.R.O. 687/23 contains 6 deeds about the mill at Avoncliff mill in Winsley, 687 /25 those for the Westwood mill.
20. K.H.Rogers, *Warp and Weft*, Barracuda Books, 1986, p.31.
21. W.A.M., Vol 21,(1892), pp 343 – 391. 'The Falstone Day Book', J.Waylen P.R.O., SP 23, vol II, Committee for Compounding, pp.497, 989. See also
WAM 23, 314 – 6.; vol 24, 58 – 103, 308 – 346. 'Wiltshire Compounders'.
22. Summary of P.C.C. wil of Michael Tidcombel, 3. August. 1662. He bequeathed
    1. To the Poor of Bradford 20s.
    2. To his wife Rebecca, annuity of £ 20 p.a. in lieu of dowry, & £20 and household stuff except best silver salt to d. Mary, & best silver bowl to Michael my youngest son.
    3. To William messuage & ten. and 1½ yard, 77½ acres 71 rood in occ of William Druce or his assigns. M. or Ten & 1½ ydland 62 acres (occ. by Thomas Baker). M. or Ten & ½ yld. 41 acres (occ A.Deverill), Roofless tenement or barn called Ashley Barne & 1 YL 49½ acres occ Joan Dick, John Dick, R.Nutt & self, former demesne lands, Merfield 30½ acres (oc. John Dick), M or Ten & 1 YL Little Ashley 50 acres, occJeremy Druce and now in my possession or assigns. Bunberie Lye (7 acres), parcel at SW end of Longman½ acre; Rowleaze 40A (Ann Long widow & John Druce); Longcroft Mead, Long Close, Broad Close, Lwr Hare knapp, Middle Close (39 A); garden plot in Bearfirld; Hareknapp in Belcombe Brook (3A); all in occ of Wm. Deverill; land and Kanlees(?) and all houses etc. belonging to the above. William to pay d. Jane £200 at 21 or marriage; & to d. Mary & youngest son Michael £200 (each?)
    4. To wife; Deverill's M or T after A.Deverill's death – but not the land.
    5. To son Edward 10 s., son Robert 20 s. Residue of goods to William..
    6. (overseers) Matthew Randolph, Thomas Baker and Richard Nutt.
    P.s. To grandchildren Jane and Ann T,d's of son Michael dec'd 20 s. each. [Are we to interpret '1½ yard 77½ acres' as a holding of nominal value 1½ yardlands and measured area 77½ acres? The '71 roods' is a mystery.]
23. Tidcombe's Will & inventory, ref. now P2/T/ 337. The site of his mercer's shop (or workshop) is not clear. It is most likely that he, like his father, as well as his widow and son, many of them clothiers, lived at Haugh Farm, the family home. But on the other hand, the will names him as 'of Bradford' – so was his shop actually in the town? Is there any evidence for a shop at Haugh?
24. Poor Rates: W.R.O. G 13/ 990 /18.

25. *Wiltshire notes and Queries*, vol vii, p.286.

26. W.R.O. 947/ 1327, dated 3 Dec 1701.

27. Two mortgages of land at Haugh Farm: W.R.O. 947 / 1340. (Feb 1723 and Apr 1725) to a mercer of Bradford.

28. One of those taking the inventory Walter Frapwell, later became tenant of the farm.

29. W.R.O. bundle 687 / 23. sale of Avoncliff Mill.

30. W.R.O. bundle 529/190.

31. Maps at W.R.O., Andrews and Dury maps are also in Wilts. Record Sos. vol 8 on a reduced scale. .Haugh Potticks Farm, no.1382 on the TA map; owner Mrs Esther Yerbury, tenant William Rose, stands on north side of road from Haugh Farm to Little Ashley

32. N.b. Upper Haugh was not sold by the Longs until the1860s.

33. John Blatchley's exchange of the Murhill land (there called Gold hill): deeds in Thresher's exchange booklet (W.R.O. 947/ 1334).

34. In W.R.O. 947/1352.

35. *W.N.& Q.*, vol viii, p.181.

36. Bristol R.O., DC / E 27 / 2 – 6. (Dean & Chapter, Manorial court books: for courts held in 1597 – 1622 by Edward Longe,see DC /E/ 27 /4. The later ones held by John Longe are in DC/ E/ 27/ 5

37. Curia Recognitionis in DC/ E/ 27/ 2; Winsley section in Appendix 3.

38. See ch.3. 'Early Houses', paragraph 2. for the wall thicknesses.

39. British Library, Egerton Ms. 3653. ut supra.

40. *Revised Medieval Latin Word-List*, Ed R.E. Latham, OUP for The British Academy, 1983

41. Curia Recognitionis.

42. The Tithe Map shows Styleclose (TA1416, 15 acres) south of Haugh Farm adjoining Parsons Hurns (TA 1415, 2 acres)

43. Bristol R.O., DC / E /3 /2; 'A Survey of the Mannor of the Rectorie of Bradford', Sept 1649.

44. W.A.M. 41, p.220.

45. Wm. Kiftill signed the Bishop's Transcripts of the Winsley parish registers, 1662-80, – apart from 1664, 1668-70. He signs himself curate in 1673, 75, 79 – 80; and 'Minister' in the rest. After that there is a gap in the transcripts till 1692; then James Butter was curate to 1704.

46. Bristol R.O. DC / E / 27 / 30: cites 21 year lease dated 3 April 4 James II (1688/9.)

47. Ib :.Articles of Agreement, Hope Long to John Hall &c., 9 Oct 1694. Summarising these grants of the Rectory, there are first the deeds of the Bradford rectory as a whole. Starting with the grant to Hope Long, from 1667 after the restoration to 1694 and the grant to John Hall after the agreement between Long and John Hall. Hall died in 1711 and the rectory passed through his descendants to Evelyn, the second Duke of Kingston. The duke died in 1773, and it appears that the Dean and Chapter soon after granted the rectory to William Clavill (Bristol Record Office, various references in whole, kept in the Dean and Chapter's ref. DC/D/ various numbers in the 200s.). The rectory of Winsley, Haugh and Holt was in turn granted by leases under the main Rector. This is told in the main text of the present chapter.

48. A. Dodge, *Freshford.* see ref 16, p. 74, etc.

49. D.N.B.; Walter Curle. There were also several generations of Walter Curles at Buttermere, Wilts.

50. Quoted in Curll's marriage settlement, at W.R.O., ref. 861 / 8..

51. Referred to as 'another deed' in W.B.R. report on Turleigh Manor, 1990. (Barbara Harvey)

52. Gloucester R.O., National Trust Dyrham archive ref. D 1799 – A 109.

53. John Curll: P.C.C. will at P.R.O.
54. The two bundles W.R.O. 947/1318/1 and 1318/2 contain among much else the Dawe papers re their rectory property in Turleigh and Winsley. The bundle also includes 947/1318/3, a very long draft of an indenture (Dawe to Thresher) dated 9 June 1733 with full details of what happened.
55. Lease (Dawe to Baskerville) in W.R.O. 947 / 1342.
56. Thresher accounts; repairs for Mr Atwood are mainly in W.R.O. 947 / 1355 etc. during the 1780s (accounts of Robert Hulbert, presumably Thresher's bailiff).
    Similarly W.R.O. 947/1349/1 tells of work at the Seven Stars in 1779 for James Broad. (carpenter's work, thatching by Aaron Pickwick etc.)
57. DC/E/ 3/4. Bristol survey of Rectory, 1788
58. DC / E / 27 / 31. Letters to the Dean from Thomas Crump and others.
59. D.N.B. article on Glass. The family seems to have lived in White Hill, Bradford, but his parents moved to Turleigh where Richard grew up.
60. Turleigh House chapel licence is in Wiltshire Record Society vol 40 *Wiltshire Dissenters' Meeting House Certificates and Registrations 1689-1852*, ed J.H.Chandler, Devizes, 1985.
61. W. R O Ref 947/1348.
62. *Wiltshire Coroners Bills, 1752 – 1796*, Ed. R. F. Hunnisett, Wiltshire Record Society, Vol. XXXVI, (1981).

Chapter 7

1. Now at the W.R.O. In most cases these transcripts date from the Constitution Canterbury in 1597, but the first surviving Winsley one is for 1622. See e.g *Enjoying Archives*, David Iredale, 1973, David and Charles.
2. There are no transcripts between 1636 and 1659. W.R. Jones, *Bradford on Avon*, p.119, analyses the confused situation of the vicarage of Bradford between the death of Rev. Thomas Reade in 1634 and the appointment of the Rev.Thomas Lewis in 1660, during which or part of which Nathanael Wilkinson may perhaps have been the vicar. Was the gap in the Winsley records perhaps related to this?
3. The Ditteridge registers contain three Winsley marriages in 1702 and 1703, two in 1704 and one in 1705. There are none either before or after these.
4. Now at W.R.O. ref. D1 /54 /6 /3.
5. In his *Gothic England* (Batsford 1947), J. H. Harvey seems to imply from the style of his work at Steeple Ashton church, that Thomas Lovell, freemason, was associated with Redman. This seems to be the closest there is to a link between the architect and Wiltshire. Harvey's book was written in 1947, leaving plenty of time for more recent discoveries to have been made.
6. Terriers dated 1608, 1678, 1794 are now at W.R.O., ref. D1/24/23/5 – 7.
7. W.R.O., will of Henry Redman, 1677.
8. *Monumental Inscriptions of Wiltshire,1822*, Sir Thomas Phillipps, Ed. Peter Sherlock, Wilts.Rec.Soc., vol.53
9. WRO deeds in ref. 947/1343.
10. See sale particulars of sale of Richard King's estate, W.R.O. ref
11. Summary in W.B.R. report. B.
12. 'Ille Terrarum Mihi Praeter Omnes Angulis Ridet'. Horace, *Odes*, book II number 6, lines 13 and 14.
13. Bristol Merchant Venturers: Information from Bristol Deposition book, vol.II: Ellacombe

Mss. (Bristol Ref. Library. and the archives at the Merchant Venturers Hall.

14. *V. C. H.* vol VII, p.17. ref.to Book of Fees 725. Cottles Atworth in 1242.

15. Bishop's Transcript, (1701) and W. R. O ref 687 / 9.

16. Cottle land on the 1727 map. Ref W.R.O. 1760 / 1H..

17. 'John Wesley and his Preachers at Bradford' W. Norman Warren. 1900.

18. Title deeds of 'Scarth', in owner's possession.

19. Several more letters from Falmouth are in reference W.R.O. 217/6

20. Calendar of Prisoners, ref. A2 / 4 / 120 – 185 at W.R.O.

21. Old church tower: see W.R.O. ref. D1 /61/6/2 .

22. W. R. O. ref. 2471 Sale particulars, 1879.

Chapter 8,

1. British Library, Egerton Ms. 3652.

2. Bowls, I presume.

3. In 1612, James Wilshere had a Hall, Kitchen, Buttery, Loft and Barn. By 1670 his son had the Hall with its chamber, the Street chamber and the next chamber, the 'overlith' chamber (is this the 'overlieth chamber, i.e. the loft?), the Middle chamber and of course the Backsyde. By 1696 the second John had added a kitchen chamber, Ground chamber, street chamber with the room under it and 'another litle chamber'. He also had the oxhouse, Backsyde, Wainhouse and the Rick Barton. Clearly some of these changes reflect the fact that those making the inventories were village worthies and not familiar with the rooms they were inspecting.

4. The first Poor Rate book, from 1702 to 1746, is at the W.R.O., ref. G 13/990/ 18. These books are an invaluable source for the ownership of the houses in the village. The oldest, a very large thick leather- bound tome, covers the years from 1702 to 1740. Its most valuable features for the present purpose are the yearly lists of the village properties, the houses, often with their land as well, with their owners and rateable values. Unfortunately it was not till much later that a particular man's property can be identified as a particular house. The houses are always listed in the same order, so one can see the owners come and go. The rateable values of the smaller properties depend only on their size, so a couple of examples will give a good idea of typical valuations. Compare Scarth, a 1d house, with the group in the village lane where the Drung meets it. At the north end, No 126 was another 1d house and 127, the small cottage between that and no 128, a ½d house. Crossing to the north side of the lane we have No.146, which was another 1d.house before its regency style east end was added about 1816, after which its rating was put up to 1½d. These small 'single rates' were not, of course, the actual sums to be paid each year on the houses. That was much larger, a multiple of this basic rate, decided annually at a meeting of the Parish vestry according to the amount the overseers required for the upkeep of those in need. For instance, in 1708 Winsley was charged in toto £57 10s, 20 times the single rate of £2.17s 6d on the whole tithing. And the figure went up astronomically during the century

5. Information from the late Mrs Moorsom given to the present owner, Capt. J Barwood. The house changed its name about 1925, according to the W.I. Scrap book.

6. The earlier deeds of no. 146 are at the W.R.O., ref. 2471.

7. The height of sill was probably 2 or 3 inches higher above the original flagged floor, which was covered and levelled for a recent wood block floor.

8. It is sometimes said that these cross boarded floors were laid in this way to keep out the smell when animals occupied the room underneath a bedroom.

9. W.A.M.41, June 1921, p.236, 'The Society's Papers', no.47a recites a trust deed of 22 March 1753, sale to John Wilshire by the Commissioners for Bankruptcy. This was in fact parsonage land. W.R.O. ref. 947 /1348 contains an indenture tripartite of 6 Dec 1748, granting this part of the 'Three Copyhold Tenements' to John Wilshere.
10. Coroner's inquisitions: see Chapter 6, ref 61.
11. W.R.O. 187/8 (and see W.R.O. 687/8) gives a list of the surviving sons and daughters of William Wilshere, a widely spread family. Besides Gould's wife Ann, Richard, (William's eldest son and heir), a yeoman of Publow, Somerset, there were three sons in law – 3 victuallers and a baker. Only Gould was still living in Winsley.
12. Reported in the *Trowbridge and N. Wilts Advertiser*, Saturday 2nd. May 1863.
13. Reports at W.B.R. office.
14. Sale particulars at the W.R.O., [sale by the exors. of Richard King, 1879]. Lot 23 was No 128, 'A substantially Built FREEHOLD DWELLING HOUSE, ... in the occupation of Mrs. King ', and Lot 24 '2 Freehold Dwelling Houses and Premises adjoining the last described Lot , (as the same is now pegged out)' Occ.by Mrs Ward (126) and Mr James Forster (127).
15. Compare Pamela Slocombe, *Wiltshire Farmhouses and Cottages 1500 – 1850*, Wiltshire Buildings Record, 1988.
16. Does this rather suggest that Nos. 126/127 were originally two buildings?
17. Map of the proposed canal in 1793 at W.R.O. Ref. A1 / 372 / 1MS.
18. The Poor Rate and Land Tax figures seem to contradict each other here. It is more likely that the Poor Rate records of the house sale were not brought up to date till 1817 – the ratepayer's name did not matter as long as the tax was actually paid.
19. Heal papers in W.R.O. ref. 33 / 137 / 1.
20. See the inventory below
21. John Lea Heal declaration in some copies of sale particulars, ref.14.
22. See ref.14 again.
23. The Bradford Omnibus.
24. This union workhouse was in the large building on the Westwood side of the Avon, to the west of the Avoncliff aqueduct
25. Methuen papers at W.R.O., ref 1742 / 4762, 21st Oct 1725.
26. Copies of all censuses that are more than 100 years old can be seen on fiche at the W.R.O. The V.C.H., vol 3 has a general discussion of the population.
27. See *The Year of the Map*, p.25.
28. Now at the W.R.O., ref. D1 / 61 / 6 / 2. It confirms that the 'Inhabitants of the said Chapelry (tithing) exceeding 2500 persons although greater number reside contiguous to the Parish Church' some 600 did live nearer to the Winsley Chapel (church). It was also specifically stated that they should convert such of the old Materials as shall be found fit for use in the new chapel. The dimensions of the new building were to be in Length 52 feet, east to west, in Breadth 30 ft, 9ins. north to south inside and the chancel 15 ft wide and 10 ft deep according to the plan attached to it.
29. Nikolaus Pevsner, *The Building of England, Wiltshire*, Penguin Books. 1963.

Appendix 1

Land exchanges: Edward Thresher and Moses Cottle.

1 29 May 1717.

[N.B. old spelling : peece or peice, feild . arr ld = arable land]
Whereas Edward Thresher is seized of:
One peice of arr land lying in the middle of Winsley's South Feild between Winsley and the Cleeves having a footpath running across the same, 166½ luggs exclusive of a piece of arr ld. adjoining thereto abutting on a piece of ground belonging to Richard Sartain not to be included in these presents.

And of two other peices of arrable adjoining the one to the other lying on the North West side of the same feild near Small Street lands, 338 luggs.

And also of one other peice of arrable in the North Feild containing one acre called or known as Dean Acre adjoining to Deanacres Path leading from Beggars Bush towards Winsley and belonging to Winsley Farm.

And Whereas Moses Cottle is seized of
One peice of arr. Land in Winsleys South Feild and shooting along after Innocks Hedge and called Huntley's, 39½ luggs·

And of one other piece of arr. in the same feild shooting by the North side of a piece of arr.ld. belonging to Edward Thresher down to Pitt Acre and containing 61 luggs.

And of one other peice of arrable ld. in the same feild called Lesters Peece with the Stripp or Neck of land adjoining leading to the Highway and containing in the whole 22 luggs

And also of one peice of arr.ld. in the same feild shooting along by the South side of the Plough Way leading to Crockford, 70 luggs.

And of one other peice of arr.ld. in the West corner of the same feild near the Grove Barriers having the land of Edward Thresher on both sides, 61 luggs.

And of one other peice of arr ld. in the same feild a little above the said Grove Barriers, 80 luggs, being parted from the said Barriers by a peice of arr. belonging to the widow Wiltshere and adjoining a peice belonging to Edward Thresher on the North side thereof.

And of one other peice of arrable, 1 acre, in Winsley's North East Feild adjoining a place called the Hillocks and near an inclosed ground called Windley belonging to Robert Parker and a yardland adjoining the North corner of Windley.

These two sets of lands to be exchanged.

Two small scraps of paper show how some of the areas were worked out, e.g.:
Mr. Thresher's land in Lower part 11 luggs
The next in length 10 lugg in breadth 4 lugg..... 40 lugg

The next 12 2 ¾ (?) 81 lugg the 2 parte 11 lugg & ½ 11½ lugg 34½ lugg) some errors here! (total) 166½ lugg) and so on

2. The same exchange was entered in abbreviated form, in Booklet 1, with the areas rewritten in Acres, Roods and Perches (luggs), e.g 166½ luggs becomes 1 acre and 6½ luggs or L 1 – 6½. Thresher's land totals 4A – 24½ L, and Cottle's 4A 2R 11½L.

3. Thresher and Cottle, 22nd Sept 1719.

Whereas Edward Thresher stands seized of and in
A peece or parcell of Arr. land called Three Acres lying in the South Feild of Winsley and shooting down the Hill near Bittam Gate and containing 2acre & ½ 34 luggs [2½A 34L]
And of and in one acre of Arr. land lying above the last mentioned peece in the sane feild and shooting across the Hill towards Youngs

And whereas Moses Cottle standeth seized of and in
A peece or parcell of arr.ld. on Gold Hill next the Conigre Wall, ½ Acre & 17 luggs
And of and in a peece or parcell of Ar.Ld lying between Bakers and Tily's containing ¼A 16 luggs
And of & in the upper end of the two lands that lyeth at the South end of the two last mencioned peeces and contayneth ¾ A and 29 luggs, all which premises were lately enclosed by the said Edward Thresher with other lands out of the same Feild which said first mencioned premises of Edward Thresher are by these presente to be exchanged and conveyed for the last mencioned premises of Moses Cottle as hereinafter mencioned.

And Whereas Edward Thresher standeth seized in and of
A close of arr. land lying at Hortly Lane end in Winsleys North Feild, 3 A(cres) 1 Q(arter) 3L(uggs)
And of and in a piece of arr. in the same feild at a place called Elingham (? Edingham) adjoining to a land of Richard Sartainon the South side thereof containing 1A 1Q. 28L.
And of & in two peeces of Arr Ld in the South Feild of Winsley called Rangens the upper peece of the said two lands, containing 227 luggs and the other peece containing 131 luggs and abutteth on the Woodlands there both whic peeces contain in the whole 2A 38L.

And whereas Moses Cottle also standeth seized of & in
A peece or parcell of arr.ld. lying the North Feild of Winsley on the lower side of the Road between Oakey and Winly (?Winsley) and adjoining to a peece of land of Edward Thresher on the South East side, 1A 2Q 21L.
And of & in one peece of arr.ld. in the same Feild lying uppon Cuccow Hhill and adjoining to a land of John Cross and abutting at the upper end upon a land of Edward Thresher on the North West end thereof, containing ½A, 28 L
And of & in another peece of arr.land lying under Baker's Tyning Wall in the same feild near the last mencioned peece, ¼ A .
And also of and in one other peece of arr.ld. in the same feild lying in a place called the Sands and adjoining to Winly hedge on the South and to the Road on the north of it, 1A½ & 3L.
And of & in one other peece of Arr. lying in the Sands adjoining to a land of William Atkins on the south east side and shooting across the Road leading from Oaky to Hortley, 64 lugg.
And of and in a peece of arrable in the same feild next Belham Stone and adjoining to a land of Edward Thresher's 47 Lugg.

And also of and in part of a land in the South Feild of Winsly near Rowhouse Shoard, 157 15ggs, being the residue of a land formerly given in exchange by Moses Cottle to Edward Thresher.

And Also of & in the upper part of three lands lying in the North Feild of Winsley, which said upper part containeth so much of the said landds as lyeth above the way leading fro Bradford to Winsley and adjoineth to a land of Edward Thresher on the South East side thereof and to the Hulks on the North East side, 145 Luggs.

Which said (last) mencioned premises of him the said Edward Thresher are also by these presents to be exchanged and conveyed for the said last mencioned premises of Moses Cottle as hereinafter.

Appendix 2

Translation of the Winsley sections of the surveys in the Shaftesbury Cartulary. [Harleian Mss. 61 at the British Library]. This translation is from Lydia M. Marshall's Latin transcription at the W. R. O. I follow her in naming the three surveys A, B, and C and her numbering of the entries. Services owed by the tenants are printed in *Italics*.

Survey A

Date, c.1132 A.D. fo. 38v. (no heading).

1. **GODWIN** 25 s. for the mill and 15 sticcas of eels and *one acre of ploughing and one of fallowing and one he reaps in August and he will lend his waggon for one day* and he will have every year one beam in the wood and the help of men and waggons for a broken mill and for bringing millstones.

2. **SCELLING** 5 s. for a virgate and a half and *he and his companion (will do) one (acre) of ploughing and one of fallowing and his waggon in August* and he goes on legation.

3. **FERMINAMUS** 4 s. (rent) and *one amber of grain* for one virgate of land.

4. **HUNELANUS** 10 s. for 1 hide (of land) and *2 acres of ploughing in winter and 2 acres fallowing in summer* and he goes to the Hundred and Shire (Sheriff's Courts).

5. **FREWINE** 4s. for half a hide *and every week one (day) a plough (- team) and a horse for carriage and 2 ambers (of grain) for Cirisset and work daily.*

6. **TODRIC** 15 d. for half a virgate.

7. **WICLAC** for one virgate and a quarter (quadranta) *and 1 amber of flour*

8. **GODWY** 20 d. for half a hide and *every week a waggon and a horse for carriage service and a days work.*

9. **ALURIC (ALVRIC)** 20 d. for half a hide and *every week a waggon and a horse for carriage service and daily work and 2 ambers of flour for Cirisset*

10. **SEWY** 39 d. for half a hide and *every week a waggon and a horse for carriage service and daily work and 1 amber of flour.*

11. **EDRIC** 6 s. for half a hide and *after this year he pays the full payments.*

12. **ELSI** 10 d. for one virgate an a half and *half a waggon every week and daily work and 1 amber of flour.*

13. **ELFRIC WITE** 15 d. for 1 virgate and *a days work and 1 amber of flour.*

14. **ULSI** 15 d. for a virgate and *every week half a plough team and half a horse and day work and one amber of flour.*

15. **ULFRIC** for 1 virgate 19 and ½ d. and he has another virgate for his Bedelry and for 2½ acres he gives 2 d.

16. **GALFRID** 5 s. for 1 virgate

17. **LEOVRIC** for half a virgate *every week 4 days work and 4 hens of Cirisset.*

18. **ELWINE TORNIOF**, similarly.

19. **SESTAN** similarly.

20. **FALGIT** similarly.

21. **ULFARD** similarly.

22. **SEMAN** similarly.

23. **ALGIT THE WIDOW** similarly except 2 hens.

24. **SCULF** and **LEOVRIC GLIDE** *do the work of one cotset, and give 8 hens.*

25. **ALWYNE** for half a virgate *works 4 days each week and gives 4 hens* and 6 d. for a small strip of land.

26. **WINSIE** for half a virgate *works 4 days in the week and gives 4 hens.*

27. **GODWINE** similarly.

28. **WLFARD** similarly for Chirisset.

29. **EDWYNE** for half a virgate *works 4 days in a week and gives 4 hens.*

30. **TODRIC** for half a virgate 18 d.

31. **SEMMANUS** similarly.

All after Galfrid except Winsie and Wlward let them each bring their burden (or financial charge?) [the latin is *ferent honera quilibet.* Honera not found in word list, but onus, pl. onera is burden, load. force, charge (in accounts)] .

32. **ELVRED** for half a hide and half a virgate 6 s. and *every week a waggon and a horse for carriage service and day work and 2 ambers of flour.*

Under Bradford the following entries in Survey A may be noted:

1. **EDWINUS PRESBYTER** has a third part of the tithes which belong to the church (of Bradford) and cemetery and the oblations of the altar and his house and 1 mansura for which he pays 12 d. and all the tithe of all the men of that mansion.
And at Atworth he has the church and 1 virgate of demesne land and all the tithes of all the men of the same Vill and must plough and fallow 1 acre.
And at Stokes he has the church and one third part of the tithes and the whole tithe of all the men of the said Vill of Stokes.

2. **PASSAT holds half a hide at TORTELEE** for 4 s. and 1 virgate which adjoins his house and 1 virgate of Wadenesdich (Wansdike) for 6 s. and several other houses and owes suit (service) to the County at his own expense. And he holds Stokes at Farm, paying 100 s. per annum and 50 s. for Toll (Tolneo) .

3. **RICHARD of the MILL** for 1 hide and for 1½ virgates he pays rent of 65 s. and 30 sticcas of eels and must plough 2 acres and fallow two acres. [Was he the earliest known member of the Hall family?]

Survey B

Date c.1166 fo. 78 – 78v.

WINESLEGA

These are the jurors of Wineslega: Roger Helda, Alvric de Wella, Reginald de Finesham.

1. **NICHOLAS DE AVENECLIFA** holds a virgate and the fourth part of a virgate and one mill for 20 s. of rent and 15 sticcas of eels and *he fallows one acre and ploughs one acre and does boon*

works.

2. **ALURIC THE MONK** 1 virgate for 4 s. of rent *and he must fallow an acre and plough and reap one and carry corn one day with his companion and do carriage service before Christmas and before Easter and carry the Lady's messages (phrase not understood) the lord's hay..*

3. **RICARDUS POWA** 1 virgate for 4 s. of rent and *carriage service the same as Alvric and besides 1 amber of corn for Chirisset and he must mow the meadow.*

4. **GODRIC HURTEMUS** one virgate for 4 s. of rent and *he fallows 2 acres and ploughs and reaps and mows daily and carries on two days.*

5. **RADULPHUS and ALFRIC** one virgate for 4 s. of rent and *they must fallow one acre and plough one and reap two and mow the meadow.*

6. **RADUS the BEDEL** half a hide for 6 s. rent and *he must fallow two acres and plough two and reap two and do carriage service before Christmas and before Easter.*

7. **REGINALD OF SIRNESHER** 1 virgate for 4 s. of rent and *fallow one acre and plough one acre and he must reap two and one amber of corn for Chirisset and mow the meadow and draw hay for two days.*

8. **REGINALD de ASLEGA** half a virgate for 15 d. of rent and *he must reap half an acre.*

9. **REGINALD the JANITOR** one hide for 10 s. of rent and *he must fallow two acres [and plough 2 acres: see A4 and C32] and pay suit at the County and Hundred (Courts)..*

10 . **COLSTAN** [presbyter at Bradford] in custodia one hide for 20 s. of rent and does nothing else but *he pays suit at the County and Hundred (Courts).*

11. **WIGANT** 2 acres and a half; *work for 2 days in one week and one day in the next and 4 hens.*

12. **RADULPHUS DE BROCA** half a virgate *for the same service.*

13. **HERDING** the same

14. **BASILIA** the same

15. **OSBERT** similarly.

16. **ACLECIA (Alecia?) the widow** half (a virgate) and *work of 3 days in one week and in the other 2 days and daily work in August (harvest) and 2 hens.*

17. **SPILEMAN** half a virgate *for the same service as Reginald (?).*

18. **HERBERT** half a virgate for *similar service.*

19. **GALFRIDUS** half a virgate *for the like service except 2 days.*

20. **HERBERT BRUT** half a virgate for 15 d. of rent and *he does daily work and cartage service once in 14 days and one amber of corn for Chirisset and half a plough (team or day?).*

21. **REGINALD the REDE** one virgate for the same service as Herbert.

22. **ALVREDUS** one virgate and ¼ of a virgate for 23 d. of rent and *let him furnish half a waggon and do carriage service once in fifteen days and one amber of corn of Chirisset and daily work.*

23. **WILLELMUS PUKE** one virgate and a half for 15 d. of rent and *he shall find half a plough one day in the week and day work and 4 hens.*

24. **WALTER KING** one virgate for 15 d. of rent and *he shall find half a wagon and one amber of corn for Chirisset and daily work.*

25. **RADUS de (AG, see C 24)** half a hide for 20 d. of rent and *in every week once, one carriage and carrying service and daily work.*

26. **ALVRED** one virgate for 15 d. of rent and *half a plough team and daily work and carrying service once a fortnight.*

27. **BRICHNOTH** one virgate for 2 s. of rent and *half a plough team in every week 1 day and work on one other day and 1 amber of corn for chirisset.*

28. **ADWARDUS** 1 virgate for the same service.

Total Rents £4. 16s. 4d.

The Abbess Cecilia gave half a hide of land to the church of Bradeford, dedicated to it and the fourth part of a virgate of land.

Survey C

Date c. 1190, no title. Fo.83 – 84

1. **JOHOBAUS [? NICHOLAUS] de AVECLIVE** holds 1 virgate of land and one mill for 20s. and for 15 stiichas of eels and *fallows and ploughs one acre.*
The same holds one half virgate of demesne land for 3 s. and for the same he leads the mill stone which the men of Wyneslegh used to bring. The same holds by villeinage the fourth part of a virgate for 12 s. (?12 d.) He shall have one tree trunk for repairing the mill and the sluice. The same goes to the demesne scot-ale as well as to the local scot-ales (scotalia vicinorum ?)

2. **ATHELINUS MONACHUS** (the Monk) one virgate for 4 s. and *he fallows and ploughs and reaps one acre and carriage service once before Christmas and once before Easter and finds one man for haymaking Muchelm(ead) and Emed (Yeamead) and half a cart for one day for hay and one day for corn and one day at the vineyard.*
The same holds one acre of demesne for 4 d. paid annually.

3. **ROGERUS PARVUS** holds one virgate for 4 s. and *fallows and ploughs and reaps one acre and at mowing and at carrying and at stacking one man daily and for one half day half a cart for the hay and likewise for the corn and at the vineyard on one day one man and for Chirecheset one bushel of grain.* (The Latin word book quotes several variants like this, all meaning church scot, ie tax, around 1200.)

4. **OSBERT of TRAUELING** half a virgate and *he works every week four days until the Nativity of St John, afterwards to the Chains of St Peter he must have every Thursday for his food one dish of grain, afterwards from the Chains of St Peter till the feast of St Michael every day one dish for his food.*

   5. **WILLELMUS HUSBUNDE**   the same.
   6. **RADUS de BROCA**   the same
   7. **ADAM de TRAVELIG** the same
   8. **WILLELMUS MONACHUS**   the same
   9. **ROGERUS de WELLE**   the same
   10. **SEWY de HAGA**   the same

11. **HELIOT de TRAUELING**   one ferleng (one farthing = ¼ virgate) *he works in one week one day and in the other week two days up to the Chains of St Peter and afterwards until the Feast of St Michael daily and he shall have daily one dish for food from the Chains to the feast of St Michael.*
The same holds one piece of demesne in the Lord's 'forunda' (Latham gives forurda = forerda = in the open field or outlying area of land)

12. **RADUS the MONK** one ferleng of land *he works in one week 2 days and in the other week 3 days until the Feast of St John and afterwards daily till the Feast of St. Michael.* The same a dish of grain like Osbert Traueling.

13. **WILLELMUS CORP** one virgate for 5 s. and *4 oxen each week and he reaps every day and he lifts by one man and half a wagon daily at the haymaking and one man for one day at stacking and every week one day half a waggon at the corn (-harvest) and he reaps one acre and one man for one day at the vineyard and carriage once before Christmas and once before Easter and for Chirisset 4 hens.*

14. **WALTER and REGINALD** half a hide except (or besides?) one ferleng for 5 s. and *6 oxen each week on one day one man at reaping and 'levandum' (haymaking or stacking?) and leading and haystack making daily and they reap one acre and do carriage service once before Christmas and once before Easter and on one day one man at the vineyard and for Chirisset one bushel of grain And if the lady wishes they shall work daily and do carriage duty in three weeks and cease in the fourth and 20 d. rent*
These men hold 3 acres of demesne to complete the 6 oxen otherwise they cannot complete them.

15. **JOHANNES BRUT** one virgate for 15 d. and *each week one day 4 oxen and carriage service every fortnight and for Chirisset one bushel of grain.*

16. **ROBERT son of GODWINE** the same.

17. **WALTER de COSSE** (perhaps Corsham) the same.

18. **ARNOLD** one virgate and one ferleng for 5 s. and *each week 4 oxen and carriage duty every fortnight and for Chirisset one bushell of wheat and if the Lady wishes he owes daily one man for work and 26 d. of rent.*

19. **ARNOLD de WROKESHAM** (Wraxall) one virgate and *each week on one day 4 oxen and when he does not find them each day one man for work and for Chirisset 4 hens.*

20. **OSBERTUS and HERBERTUS** one virgate for 4 s. and *each week on one day two oxen and for Chirisset one bushel, (and) daily one man at reaping and haymaking (levandum) and leading in and making the stack and they shall reap one acre and at the vineyard one man for one day.*

21. **RICARDUS PUCHE** one virgate of Demesne for 5 s. and *he reaps two acres and one man at Muchm. and at Emed one man and at the stacking one day one man and at the vineyard one day one man.*

22. **ROGERUS WIGANT** one virgate for 15 d and *4 oxen for one day of each week and for each fortnight carriage duty and whenever he does not do this one man works every day.*

23. **ROBERTUS de CUNBERWELL** half a hide and a ferleng of land for 7 s. and carriage *in preparation for Christmas and twice before Easter and he will fallow and plough and reap two acres and one man for one day at the vineyard and one wagon for one day at haymaking and on one day at the ripe corn and one man at the haymaking of Muchelmead and one man at Emed and one man at stacking the hay..*

24. **RADUS de AG'** half a hide for 20 d. and *each week one cart and carriage duty each week and when he does not do this, daily one man at labour.* The same holds 4 acres of demesne and one acre of meadow to make up his half hide.

25. **ALVRED de HAG'** one virgate of vileinage and a half a virgate of demesne for 15 d. *and each week on one day 4 oxen and each fortnight carriage and when he does not do it each day one man at work and fort Chirisset 4 hens.* The same holds 1 ferleng of the lands from Walter and Roger de Wirlesleg (? Winesleg') to complete his virgate.

26. **RICARDUS de HAG'** half a virgate and *he works 3 days each week until the feast of St John and afterwards daily until the feast of St Michael and he shall have for his meal each Thursday one dish of grain from the feast of St John until the Chains of St Peter and afterwards one dish daily and for Chirisset 4 hens.*

27. **ROBERT DETH** similarly [Possibly Deth is De A(twr)th].

28. **ROGERUS de HAGA** one virgate of villeinage and half a virgate of demesne for 15 d. and *each week 4 oxen for one day and carriage each fortnight and for Chirisset 4 hens. And if he does not do this, each day one man at work.*

29. **EDWARDUS de XERNESHAM** one virgate for 4 s. and *he fallows and ploughs and reaps one acre and one man at the mowing and one man at the haymaking and one man and one horse for the leading in from Muchelmed and Emed and at the stacking one man and cartage once before Christmas and once before Easter and for Chirisset one bushel of wheat.*

30. **EDWARDUS and WILLELMUS** half a hide for 4 s. and *each week on one day one waggon and cartage each week and when they do not do this one man each day for work and for Chirisset 2 bushels of wheat.*

31. **WALTER de HASLEGH** (Ashley) half a virgate for 15 d. and *one man at the haymaking at Muchelmd and Emed and at the stacking and he reaps on one day half an acre and receives 'copsef' (?) and at the vineyard one day.*

32. **MAGISTER HAM** one hide for 10 s. and he *fallows and ploughs 2 acres* and he goes to the County at his Tourn (the sheriff's Tourn). The same holds of demesne in one his ley one 'helam'

(? all in one piece).

33. **WILLELMUS de BUDDEBERE** one hide for 20 s. and he goes to the County at his tourn. The same holds of demesne one furlang in the west part of Wixilages. The same and Magister Ham will go to the scot-ale of the Lady as well as to the local scot-ale.

All others at the Lady's scot-ale 3½ d.

For toll (Tholoneum?) per annum 8 s. For sheriff's aid 40 d.

All those who mow and spread the hay meadow shall have 15 d. and two sheep when it is finished in any year.

At 'laqueritia' all those who find each week one cart shall have their meal or two halfpence

The Bedel shall have one acre of wheat for his pay and 'budelstiches' and one sedlep of wheat for Christmas and one sedlep at Easter because it is sown after ploughing. The same shall have each day one 'deisef' each day on the chief harvest until the whole has been led in and (he shall) guard them by day and by night and shall pay rent without amerciament two for one if any is stolen or destroyed by pack horses.

Appendix 3

Translation of the Winsley section of the Curia Recognitionis minutes, Bristol R.O. DC/ E 27/ 2.

Court of Acknowledgement of all and singular the customary tenements which are held by Indenture with a survey of all and singular their lands, tenements and hereditaments by which they belong to the said Prebend and in what way the tenants hold each individual holding aforesaid. Taken at Bradford the 9th day of December in the fifth year of the reign of the Lady Elizabeth (1563),

Wyndeslegh

James Baenes is acknowledged to hold by Copy (of Court Roll) made to the same James, his wife, and their son John, dated the 28th day of September in the second year of the reign of King Edward the sixth (1548), One messuage with its appurtenances in Turley formerly in the tenure of John Davis. He owes heriott when it arises. And there is licence for the same James to substitute a subtenant to him and he pays £3 per annum.

The same James is acknowledged to hold by another copy made to the same James, dated 28th April in the 29th year of Henry Viii (1536) one cottage and half a virgate and 8 acres of land with its appurtenances in Winneslie formerly in the tenure of John Crynne. Not (subject to) heriott. Rent £4.

William Guiding holds by copy of the Court dated 12th January, 5th Edward VI, by grant of Richard Tourgen (Tourgey?) then the Steward (of the court) a tenement and a close of 2 acres of pasture adjacent to it called Murrells with divers other closes of (arable) land and pasture adjacent to the same in Windeslegh aforesaid, to have (and to hold) to him and William his son. Rent £3 yearly.

David Atkyns holds by Copy dated 16th May, 17 Henry VIII (1525) in the time of the Abbess of Shaston one Messuage and half a virgate of land with its appurtenances in Hawy (Haugh) in the tithing of Wyneslegh Viz(?) of one messuage [the next two lines of the manuscript are badly damaged]...two fallows(?) .... lying in the .... land in the Mead(?) in the Westfield, two acres in the Eastfield at (? a place called) 'Hillared Hyll' (probably Shillards) and another parcel of meadow and pasture land containing by estimation 14 acres, To hold to him for his lifetime at an annual rent of 3s. 4d. for the premises, granted by Richard Toutgen, at that time the Farmer there. (for the lives of (?)) Richard Atkyns , John Atkyns 30 nt(?) by copy made to them there dated 10 Jan,

6 Edward VI by convertion(?) of one messuage and a virgate of land for a fine of 30d.

Anna Wilshere widow holds for her wodowhood a messuage and a virgate of land with appurtenances in Wyneslegh aforesaid, viz a close, a garden etc. lying at the back of the said tenement containing a rood of land

A close of pasture called Gelestyche containing 2 acres
A close called Norwoods Close, 2½acres
A close called Styleclose, 2 acres
A close called Barnes containing, 3 acres
Brodecrofte 3 acr.
Pedes (or Peredes)   2 acres
Wurnygsheclose 2 acres
Elkeborough 2 roods
Crockeforde close 2 acres
Lowley ½ acre
Rowweys 2½ acres
Okeweyes 1 vigr (?)
One detached strip of meadow called Bradleys Mead, 1 rod.
12 acres of (Arable) land in Westfelde with apps. and 12 Acres in the Northfelde
To hold to her and her son William for a yearly rent of 20 s.

Henry Rogers, gent. holds by Copy dated 4 Nov, 25 Henry VIII, containing land, meadow and pasture called Stertes with all its appurtenances lying and being in the tithing of Wynselegh ...

The reversion there was granted (by? or to?) John Webbe Antony Webbe and William Webbe the sons of William Webbe of Bradforde aforesaid formerly (defactus) by Copy dated the.... day of April 6 Edward VI, to be held by them successively for the terms of their lives....

Tenants by Indenture
Wynesley   Richard Wyllowes holds there by Indenture dated 3 Sept. 38
Henry VIII under the seal of the Dean and Chapter of Bristol, the Rectory of Hawght in Wyneslegh and also all lands meadows and pastures containing by estimation ... seven illegible words....] with all and singular its appurtenances belonging to the said Rectory together with all Tithes of grain, hay and lambs with all other fruits belonging to the foresaid chapel of Wyneslegh. To have and to hold to himself, Edith his wife and John his son for the term of their lives. And the foresaid Richard, Edith and John shall well and sufficiently repair and maintain all the premises in all necessary repairs during the aforesaid term. And the Clause of re-entry for non payment of the rent 'sidcus(?)' he will pay back the unpaid rent at the rate of one month after three at each Feast of each Feast for which he shall be in debt.......

Appendix 4

Inventory of goods and chattels distrained by George Butt Tithingman of Winsley Wilts the property of Mr Ambrose Heal by virtue of the annexed warrant under the hands of Thomas Tugwell & John Long Esquires two of His Majesty's Justices of the peace for the County of Wilts this 11th day of September 1820 for the Sum of £182.4.9 as follows

1st Kitchen
4 Tables
Scales & Waits
Oak Bureau
2 Tables
Clock in oak case
7 Chairs
6 Prints
Sundry ware
3 Waiters & Tea caddy
10 Books
2 Doz Blue ware
2 Sets of Tea '
20 Glasses
Knives Forks & Box & Salt Box
Copper coffee pot and cap
6 Brass candle sticks
4 Iron Flats
Brass Trivett Pepper Box
Sundry ware
Fire Irons Fender & Grate
12 Silver table spoons
6 Tea '
1 Pair Sugar Tongs

2nd Kitchen
1 Stone Bacon Sitt
Boiler & Grate
1 Pigh Stone
Scales & Waits
2 Tables
4 Chairs
1 Steel Fender

Sundry ware
1 Barrell

Back Yard
5 Iron bars 2 Sledges & other
    Quarry tools
1 Iron Pott 1 Copper Kettle

Bed Room No 1
1 Flock Bed & 2 Bolsters
2 Blankets
Tent Bed Stead & Furniture
5 Chairs
Washing Stand basin, etc
3 Prints & ornaments
Side Carpets

Bed Room No 2
Oak post Bedstead
Flock Bed & Bolster
2 Sheets 1 Quilt & 1 Blanket
Crib Bed bolster Blanket & 2
    Sheets
Night Table
Oak chest of Drawers
2 Pair of Sheets
4 Boxes
2 Chairs
Window curtains
Side Carpets

Stair base
Stair Carpet & Cloth

Bridle & Saddle
4 Sacks
Stone Grate

1st Garrett
5 Stone saws
10 Bords & Sundry

2nd Garrett
1 Stump Bedstead
Flock Bed & Bolster
2 Sheets & Quilt
Sundrys

Yard
8 Ligh Stones
2 Carts
Block Ashler Tile & Bricks
Wood
Stone Draugh & Grind Stone
3 Barrows

Stable
2 Horses & Harness
1 Mare & Colt in the Field
3 Pigs

Hay in the yard and in Daggers
    Field
Quantity of block and other
    Ashler at the Quarry
At the wharf 2 loads of block &
    other Ashler

Index

Over Westwode 41
Oxen Sitting 82

Parfitt, Rev.C. 76
Parsonage Farm 23, 44, 89, 91
Passet 26
Perry, Scudamore, 95
Pickwick, Aaron 74, 87, Moses (I,II,III) 87, 88
Pombury 40
Pond, village 39
Ponting, Robert 52, Thomas 50
Poteck, Ralph 86
Potticary, Jerome, Ann 67
Potticks House 86
Pound, the 119

Rackhams 83
Radus (bedel) 36
Rance family 103
Reade, Kathrine 67
Redman, Henry 101-103, Thomasina (m. Wilshere) 102
Rednans House, Burghope 99
Reginaldus de Ashley 30, de Legh 30
Robin Hoods Bay 118
Rock House (Scarth) 116
Rowas, Rowhays 16, 21, 90
Rowbarrow 18, 19, 22
Rowley 40

Saccon 29
Saleman Philip 38
Sally in the Woods 71
Sally Port 21
Sands, the 61
Saunders, Thomas Hosier 127
Says Green 80
Scarth 47, 109, 116, 117, 118, 121, 122
Scotland 21
Selwood forest 33
Semington 56
Seven Stars 8. 74. 79. 87. 103. 103
Seven Stars, Newtown 79
Shaa, Robert 82
Shaftesbury Abbey 4, 24, 13, 24, 27, 31, 32, 34, 37, 44, 50, 53, 64, 65, 88, 105

Sheepstails 15, 18
Shilhorn 21
Sidney, Philip 65
Skull. Adam 87
Smallcombe, Joseph 12, 127
Smyth, John 37
Sofa Stone 21
Southbroom 55
South Stoke 92
South Wraxall 1, 64, 86, 102
Southwick 41
Stapeley 12
Staindrop (Durham) 115
Stamborough 18
Staverton 34, 55
Sterts, Serts Lane 21, 54, 59, 91
Stevens, William 55
Stoke 2, 37, 57; (Limpley) 1, 26; parsonage 9
Stoke, Stokesford bridge 16, 126
Stone, William 113, 114
Stoneleigh 121
Strickland, Sir William 91
Stubb Leaze 18
Summerlugg 21
Sutcliffe School 107
Swan Hotel, Bradford 129
Swett Close 21

Tatlor, William 9
Tawstock 73
Tedzells 21
Temple Ground (Eastcroft) 20
Thorntelegh, Torteleg' 26, 30
Thresher, Edward 71-73, , John 6, 71-73, 96, family 74, 75, 87
Tidcombe, Edward 81-84, Michael 81-85
Tory 79
de Traveling family 4
Tourgen(?) William 53
Trowbridge 28, 43
Trowle 1, 30, 31
Trows 24, 61
Turgey (?=Tourgen), Bartholomew 101
Turleigh 56, 57, 60, 93, 94 96, 97, 112, 121
Green Lane 49, 67

Ulf 225, 29

Ulfric 29
Underwood, Guy 22
Uplands 93, 118
Upper Haugh Farm 82, 87

Vennell family, William 62, 63
Vennells (No 141, Winsley) 62

Walsingham, Sir Francis 65, 66, 89, Frances 66
Warley 22, 24
Warnage 73, 90
Wayfer, Robert 33
Webbe, William 66, 88, Richard 101
Wellclose 79, 82
Westbury 41
Westbury(alias Reynolds), John 54, 55, Richard 51, William 55
Westwood 24, 27, 41
Weyhill 70
Wheatsheaf 89, 103
Whippe, John 61
Whitley 118
Wiclac 28
Willys, Richard 51, 89
Wilshere (Wylshyre), Henry 43, James 61, Joan 42, John 6, Richard 71, Thomas 42
Wimborne St Giles 41
Wine 3
Wine Street 78, 79, 80
Wingfield 40
Winley 34, 35
Winsley Croft, House 60, 73
Winterslow 47
Withy John 57
Woolley 24, 25, 26, 31
Wraxall, South 26, 28, 36, 37, 116, 121, 122, 131, 132
Wrey, Sir Bourchier, 73
Wyvil, Robert, Bishop of Sarum 34
de Wynsele, William 33

Yeamead, Eamed 21
Yerbury, Francis 83, 85, John 80, Walter 79
Yewe, John 79
Yonge, Thomas 39